Stick With It
How to Overcome the Obstacles
That Keep You from Following Through

Greg Wingard

Stick With It™

How to Overcome the Obstacles That Keep You from Following Through

PINNACLE
BUSINESS
PRESS

Greg Wingard

First Edition

Wingard, Greg 1963
Stick With It™/Greg Wingard

ISBN 09777967-0-1
1. Success 2. Sales 3. Management
I. Title

Editor Dan Johnson
Cover design by Son Duong (sonduong@comcast.net)
Text Layout and production by Roberta Great (greatgraphics@charter.net)

10 9 8 7 6 5 4 3 2 1

DEDICATION

To our children, Moriah and David.
May you carry into adulthood the wonderful persistence
you demonstrate now.

WELCOME FRIEND!

I am thrilled you are holding this book in your hands! I am passionate about helping people grow in their personal and professional lives and I greatly appreciate the opportunity to make the journey with you.

What we *prize* most *costs* the most. Prizes—whether enduring relationships, thriving careers, excellent health, or financial well-being – require time, energy and stamina to win.

Every page of this book has been crafted to help you overcome the obstacles that keep you from following through, so you can achieve what matters most to you.

As we progress together you will see that I am sharing with you as a fellow learner. Like you, I'm continually learning and growing. Therefore, you will find the ideas in this book *practical*—rather than theoretical. And you will find the tone *encouraging*—rather than overwhelming. I want this book to be the most *practical, useful,* and *encouraging* resource you've ever discovered to help you follow through and achieve what matters most to you.

So let's grow together. Let's build our stamina. Let's stick with it and go to the next level in our lives!

How to get the most from *Stick With It*

1. Take what works and leave the rest. View the insights here as a smorgasbord from which to choose.

2. Focus on incremental improvement. The applications in the book will take only a few minutes to do, enabling you to digest the material and move forward in small, doable steps.

3. Mark it up. Use it as a journal and make it your own.

4. For salespeople, each chapter includes a "Quick Tip for Sales Professionals." If you manage a sales team, these will provide excellent material for coaching conversations.

5. Celebrate your forward-movement. Don't beat yourself up over what you *don't do*. Feel great about every bit of positive progress you make!

THE 21 STRATEGIES

Part 1 Overcoming Distraction

1 **LONG-TERM:** Be patient and think long-term 3

2 **FOCUS:** Decide what to focus on right now 11

3 **SAY NO:** Increase your impact by saying "No" 19

4 **ACT:** Do something now 27

5 **NOW:** Stay in the *now* 35

6 **SELF-COMPETE:** Compete with yourself 43

7 **ENVIRONMENT:** Build an environment that supports you 49

Part 2 Overcoming Inertia

8 **PURPOSE:** Anchor your goals to deeper purpose 59

9 **FIRE:** Fire yourself up by making your goals more compelling 67

10 **IDEAS:** Discover ideas that help you improve 73

11 **SMALL IMPROVEMENTS:** Make small, incremental improvements 81

12 **MOMENTUM:** Turn your wins into winning streaks 89

13 **HABITS:** Get better one habit at a time 95

14 **BIG CHANGE:** Make a big strategy change when necessary 103

Part 3 Overcoming Discouragement

15 **MOODS:** Manage your moods 113

16 **EXPECT:** Expect to prevail 121

17 **BE REALISTIC:** Be realistic about how long it takes 129

18 **USE FAILURE:** Use failure to move forward 137

19 **SELF-TALK:** Improve your self-talk 143

20 **ENERGY:** Give yourself the energy to follow through 153

21 **KEEP SWINGING:** Keep swinging your bat 161

THE THREE OBSTACLES

You set an exciting goal. You were energized by it. You charted a course and started working toward it. But along the way, your progress slowed and you didn't follow through. What started with a bang ended with a whimper.

Why does this happen? Why is it so difficult to follow through? And most importantly, what can we do to finish strong?

That's the point of this book. Together we will explore the three obstacles to follow through and 21 strategies to overcome them. The strategies are not *steps*. You don't need to employ all of them. Any single strategy could be the one that helps you over the hurdle. So again, take what works for you.

First, let's identify the three obstacles:

1. Distraction
We're pulled in *so many directions*. When we set a goal, we choose a course and start working toward it. But we face many distractions along the way that can lead us off course. The first seven strategies will help you overcome distraction and stay focused on your goals.

2. Inertia
A rocket uses most of its fuel in the first few minutes of flight. So it is in reaching our goals. To achieve new results, we must break out of the inertia of old behaviors, attitudes, and patterns. It takes a lot of fuel to break through inertia. The second seven strategies provide more rocket fuel to get into a higher orbit of living.

3. Discouragement

The path to goal achievement can be tough! There are many things we encounter that can discourage us and tempt us to quit. The final seven strategies will help you deal with discouragement constructively so you stick with it until you win the prize.

Part 1

OVERCOMING DISTRACTION

Do you know why a lion tamer uses a chair to subdue the lion? Because a lion can't focus on multiple points of the chair simultaneously. The inability to focus on a single point immobilizes the lion.

It's the same for us. When we have too much coming at us, we shut down. We throw up our hands and say, "What's the use?" In our day, when we feel pulled in many directions, it takes uncommon focus to sustain the action needed to achieve our goals.

The first seven strategies will help you exert that uncommon focus so you can achieve *your* most important goals.

Stick With It

LONG-TERM

Be patient and think long-term

"We tend to over-estimate what we can do in the *short-term*
and under-estimate what we can do in the *long-term*."

Rick Warren

We hate to wait!

Most of us are impatient about getting results. It *is difficult* to
maintain long-term perspective as we work toward our goals.

Let's face it! You and I have grown up with fast food, microwave
ovens, mobile phones, and instant messaging. Everything we
experience says, "Get what you want *right now*."

Big prizes require investment over time

But big prizes take time to achieve. Exciting career goals, deep
and lasting relationships, and excellent health take time, energy,
and stamina to achieve.

There is no such thing as "instant results" with these bigger
prizes.

You have what it takes

You and I have what it takes to achieve our goals. We really do. It's easy to get stuck in self-limiting beliefs. But please don't!

Study after study has proven that the most important quality in goal-achievement is a *long-term perspective*. It trumps education, family background, and even IQ.

In 1921, Stanford University began a study of 1,528 gifted children. The goal was to uncover the relationship between intelligence and achievement. The surprising result was that IQ is *not* the most important predictor of success. Stanford discovered that self-confidence, perseverance, and a tendency to set goals were far more important.[1]

Harvard study confirms it

Those findings have been repeated over and over.

In 1979, Harvard University studied their MBA graduates. Upon completion of their MBA, students were asked, "Have you set clear, written goals for your future and made plans to accomplish them?" Only 3% had written goals and plans. Another small group, 13%, had unwritten goals. The remaining 84% simply wanted to finish school and enjoy the summer.

Ten years later researchers reconnected with the students. Here's what they found: the 13% with unwritten goals were earning, on average, twice as much as their counterparts without goals. And what about the 3% with written goals and plans? They were earning more than the entire remaining 97% of the class *combined.*[2]

The evidence is overwhelming. Long-term thinking is the most important quality in achieving goals. This is a *perspective held in the mind*—so it is something that can be possessed *right now*.

Three ways to think long-term about our daily actions

Plutarch said, "Many things which cannot be overcome when they are taken together, yield themselves up when taken little by little." Here are three ways to view daily activities with a long-term perspective:

1. Lay a stone
Every action we take today is like laying a stone.

Stone by stone we're building the tower of our life. Earl Nightingale uses a building metaphor in his *Lead the Field* program:

"A lifetime is comprised of days, strung together into weeks, months, and years. Let's reduce it to a single day, and then, still further, to each task of that day. A successful life is nothing more than a lot of successful days put together… Think of a single day as a building block with which you're building the tower of your life. Just as a stonemason can put only one stone in place at a time, you can live only one day at a time… Now each day consists of a series of tasks—tasks of all kinds. And the success of a day depends upon the successful completion of most of these tasks. If everything we do during the day is a success—that is, done in the best fashion of which we're capable—we can fall asleep that night in the comfortable knowledge that we've done our very best, that our day has been a success, that one more stone has been successfully put into place." [3]

There is a legend about two brick masons who toiled side by side in a massive building project that had been under construction for years. One of the men grumbled and complained daily. The other man remained cheerful despite the grueling work. One day the grump insisted that the other man explain how he could remain happy moving and laying heavy stones day after day. His answer was simple, "As you work, all you see are the stones you lay. As I work, *I see the cathedral we are building.*"

Every action we take today is laying another stone in place. We are building the tower of our life. We musn't lose sight of that. As we keep that compelling vision before us, it infuses what we do today with fresh energy and purpose.

> "*My success evolved from working hard at the business at hand every day.*"
> Johnny Carson

2. Plant a seed
Every action we take today is a planted seed that will produce a future harvest.

This idea is based on the timeless principle that "what a person sows, they also reap." As 21st century people, we intellectually *know* this principle, but we have trouble *thinking this way.*

The principle of sowing and reaping includes an unspoken 'between' stage spelled w-a-i-t-i-n-g. The farmer knows that seeds planted during one season will produce a harvest in another, *even though there is a period of incubation where progress is being made even when it's not seen.*

Thinking long-term about what we do each day means seeing our actions as seeds of a future harvest. Even though we can't see the result of today's action immediately, we must recognize that what we do today will produce future results.

3. Move the ball down the field
Every action we take today moves the ball down the field toward

the goal line.

In football, breakaway plays bring crowds to their feet. But most plays are short-yardage gains. Rather than relying on the breakaway play to reach our goals, we want to take the long-term view: "I will reach my goal by continually moving the ball down the field."

Consider these examples of moving the ball down the field:

- Sales growth occurs one new sale a time.
- Skill improvement occurs one new skill at a time.
- Weight comes off one pound at a time.
- Net worth grows one dollar at a time.

Writer Roald Dahl, author of *Charlie and the Chocolate Factory*, captured the discipline it takes to keep moving the ball down the field when he said, "I start at 10 o'clock and I stop at 12. Always. However well I'm going, I will stay there until 12, even if I'm a bit stuck. You have to keep your bottom on the chair and stick it out. Otherwise, if you start getting in the habit of walking away, you'll never get it done."

> *"When I have finally decided that a result is worth getting, I go ahead on it and make trial after trial until it comes."*
> Thomas Edison

Every action taken today moves the ball down the field toward the goal line. Value the small yardage gains. Value the new account you brought on. Value the new skill you developed. Value the pound you lost. Value the dollar you saved. Yard by yard, keep moving the ball down the field.

QUICK TIP FOR SALES PROFESSIONALS

Always agree on a "next step" with your prospects.

What percentage of the time do you "move the ball down the field" with your prospects by agreeing on a next step? _____ %

What single change can you make *today* to increase that percentage?

_____

_____

_____

APPLY: Where do you want to be in one year?

Select one area in your personal life and one area in your professional life. Now project yourself 12 months into the future. Think about what you would like to achieve and where you would like to be. Remember, people tend to over-estimate what can be accomplished in the short-term, but under-estimate what can be accomplished in the long-term.

Where do I want to be one year from now in my **personal life?**

_____

_____

_____

_____

Where do I want to be one year from now in my **professional life?**

_____

_____

_____

_____

_____

Most goals are achieved, if we simply follow through

Brian Tracy cites a study on goal orientation that found 95% of the goals set by participants were ultimately achieved, as long as they persisted.[4] Think long-term. Lay your stone, plant your seed, and move the ball down the field, confident that what you do today is moving you closer toward the results you want tomorrow.

Stick With It

FOCUS
Decide what to focus on right now

"Whatever you focus on you move toward."
Anthony Robbins

We have endless possibilities available to us
One of the great things about being alive today is the endless possibilities available. But that's also one of the great challenges.

It is difficult to choose the great over the good. But to achieve goals, *one must choose.*

> *"There are 50,000 ways for me to make money. But if I try to make money 50,000 ways, I won't make money at any of them."*
> Zig Ziglar

Zig Ziglar says, "There are 50,000 ways for me to make money. But if I try to make money 50,000 ways, I won't make money at *any* of them."

The same could be said about achieving our goals.

There are 50,000 goals we could achieve right now. But if we don't focus on *a few* of them, we won't achieve *any* of them.

To overcome the distraction of endless possibilities, the ability to focus must be developed. *Focus can begin right now!*

Three benefits of focus

When someone decides what to focus on right now, it has an amazing effect. Bill Cosby said, "Anyone can dabble, but once you've made that commitment, your blood has that particular thing in it, and it's very hard for people to stop you." Specifically, focus helps us in three ways:

1. Focus tunes out distraction

By deciding what to focus on right now, other distractions are tuned out.

In high school, I had a coach who taught us this principle as it related to shooting the basketball. When we were shooting, he instructed us to identify and aim for one of the *rings* on the hoop rather than merely the hoop itself. The act of locating and focusing on a *single ring* forced the shooter to tune out the distractions of everything else.

When you and I decide what to focus on right now, the same thing happens. Identifying and focusing on a few top goals tunes out the distractions of all the other good possibilities.

2. Focus ignites us to act

Focus rouses us and ignites us to act. Before focus, we can feel paralyzed by inaction.

In the romantic film comedy, *Ever After,* the prince is reawakened to a life of purpose by an idealistic and beautiful commoner. One evening, the prince gets a vision to start a university in his medieval Paris that would be open to all. As he excitedly shares his vision, he says, "I used to think that if I did *something*, I'd have to do *everything*, and then I'd go stark raving mad!" It was when he realized he didn't need to do everything—but instead something—that he was ignited to act.

Bill and Melinda Gates have given more than $20 billion dollars to their non-profit foundation. Their devotion to philanthropy is truly remarkable. Yet, *even they* must focus their efforts. Their foundation *concentrates* its effort in specific areas of healthcare and education.

Like the Gateses, Oprah Winfrey is making a big difference through focused effort. And like the Gateses, she is motivating others along the way to do what they can.

Oprah appeared on David Letterman's show in late 2005. The late-night comedian was unusually reflective, probing Oprah about her work in Africa. When Dave lamented the immense challenges facing the continent, Oprah passionately encouraged him. She told Dave not to be overwhelmed by the problem. Instead, Oprah said, we should all figure out what we can do and do our part.

It is intensely liberating to realize that we don't have to do *everything*—but can choose *something* that is deeply meaningful and highly impactful.

Deciding what to focus on right now ignites us to act.

3. Focus magnifies our effort

By deciding what to focus on right now, effort is magnified.

Consider the example of a karate punch. The power of the punch comes from the *focus* of the punch. A small person can break bricks with a focused punch.

Consider the example of a laser. The power of a laser comes from the *focus* of light. Steel can be cut with focused light.

Consider the example of Julius Caesar.

On January 1, 49 B.C., Julius Caesar made a decision that changed history. With the words, "the die is cast," he crossed the Rubicon River with his army, declaring civil war against Pompey and headed straight for Rome.

Pompey had a strong upper hand. He had the power, position and a greater army. Caesar was outmatched in every way—except one. Caesar took decisive, focused action. He knew what he wanted and went straight for it.

Caesar's power came from the *focus* of his effort. Pompey's larger forces were defeated through Caesar's focused effort.

Likewise, one can "break bricks," "cut through steel," and win when outmatched by circumstances through a focused effort. Focus *magnifies* effort.

How to focus

Earl Nightingale, one of the great student/teachers of achievement, distinguished between two types of people: *river* people and *goal* people. *River* people are the lucky few who seem to know early in life exactly what their purpose is and they easily swim within that river all of their lives. The rest of us are *goal* people. We discover and fulfill our purpose by setting and achieving goals. We *choose to focus.*

Here are some practical ways to decide *what to focus on right now.* Use this two-step process to establish goals for a year or a quarter. Use this process to establish top takeaways from a convention or seminar. Use this process when you finish this book.

1. Create a Top Ten Ideas List

The first step is to capture all of the great possibilities. If you are setting goals for a quarter or for a year, begin the process by creating a Top Ten Ideas List of great goals you'd like to consider.

In the same way, if you are synthesizing the material from a seminar, distill the ten best ideas you generated that you would like to consider for action.

Capture everything. Have fun with this.

2. Choose the Top Three Actions

After capturing the ten best ideas, narrow down your list to a Top Three Actions List.

This is more difficult to do than creating the Top Ten Ideas List. It requires the discipline of selection. But this step is critical. To focus, one simply must say "No" to most of the great ideas available

> *"Stop complaining or feeling sorry for yourself about what you don't have, and instead, ask yourself what you truly want!"*
> Erin Brockovich and M. Eliot

to them. No one can do everything. No one can even do *most* things. But a *few things* can be done very well.

In the book, *Execution*, Larry Bossidy and Ram Charan make the point that if someone identifies ten priorities, the hard work is yet to be done. They strongly believe that people can only focus on three or four priorities at a time.[1]

This is exactly how General Electric achieved its unbelievable success over the past two decades. In his book, *Winning*, former

CEO Jack Welch stressed that the direction he took General Electric was a *focused choice.* GE successfully executed on its *chosen strategy,* but it could have gone a number of other directions and been equally successful. GE couldn't do it all. Even a top level company had to focus and then execute on the plan.[2]

Resist the temptation to overreach. Power is in *focused effort.* This requires the discipline of saying "No" to most great opportunities and giving full effort to the most important ones.

QUICK TIP FOR SALES PROFESSIONALS

Give more attention to your best opportunities.

Identify your most important client, prospect, and new opportunity. After you have done that, ask yourself this simple question, "Am I giving them as much focus as I should right now?" If not, what will you do to give them the focus they deserve?

CLIENT _____

PROSPECT _____

OPPORTUNITY _____

APPLY: Choose now!

New York Yankee star, Derek Jeter, said, "If you don't set goals, you're not going to have dreams, either. The goals are the achievements along the way to get you to your dreams…The longer you wait to decide what you want to do, the more time you're wasting."

If you are distracted by the many good possibilities available to you, choose *now* and put the potency of focus to work for you.

Top Ten Ideas List:

1. _____

2. _____

3. _____

4. _____

5. _____

6. _____

7. _____

8. _____

9. _____

10. _____

Top Three Actions List (What? By when?):

1. _____

2. _____

3. _____

Stick With It

SAY NO

Increase your impact by saying "No"

"If you chase two rabbits, both will escape."

Unknown

Say "Yes" by saying "No"

To say "Yes" to the most important goals, one must to say "No" to all the other *great opportunities* that come along. William James said, "The art of being wise is the art of knowing what to overlook."

A gardener must continually prune plants and pull weeds because, left alone, *the garden will become overgrown and unproductive*. To overcome distractions that demand attention, saying "No" is required.

> *"Today's workplace demands that you focus not just on what's merely important, but on what's wildly important."*
> Stephen Covey

Because of constant daily distractions, *uncommon focus is necessary to reach important goals*. Maintaining this uncommon focus requires continually saying "No" to everything else. Constant pruning and weeding is in order to assure that our "plants" are healthy and productive.

Get over the guilt

So many good things shout for attention and threaten false guilt if left behind. Yet it is simply *not possible* to do everything we feel we *should* do.

Several years ago I asked a friend, then an executive at a Fortune Fifty company, how work was going. His face reacted before he spoke. He said, "I have 73 priorities. *Seventy-three!* It's absolutely crazy." It *is* crazy. He told me the only way he could be productive was by ignoring the least important 60 "priorities."

It's that way for each of us. Achieving excellence in *some* areas requires ignoring other areas and eliminating the false guilt that comes from saying "No" to other good things.

How to say "No"

In *Good To Great*, Jim Collins points out that, "The good-to-great companies at their best followed a simple mantra: 'Anything that does not fit... we will not do.'"[1] Here are three important ways to increase impact by saying "No:"

1. Say "Stop" to that which is no longer worth doing

Much human activity is unnecessary. People create "to do" lists all the time. When was the last time you intentionally created a "stop doing" list?

This is an important way to create time and space for other, more valuable activities.

Oscar-winning actress Helen Hunt acknowledged the importance of this when she said, "…the only time I've moved forward in my career is when I had the courage to say 'No' to things that were safe or that I'd done before, in order to create space for something new to enter."

Here are some questions to ask in creating your own "stop doing" list:

- What am I doing that has lost its original impact?
- What am I doing that is good, but not good enough to justify continuing?
- What am I doing that I should do *less* of?
- What am I doing that I should discontinue immediately?

APPLY

Do this: give yourself the gift of having less to do. By saying "Stop" to unnecessary tasks, space is created for new ideas that will be more forwarding to your goals.

"Stop Doing" List:

1. _____

2. _____

3. _____

4. _____

5. _____

2. Say "Later" to things worth future consideration

One of the ways to say "No" is by saying "Later" to good things that merit future consideration.

Today's great ideas may become top priorities later. Those ideas can be valuable when the timing is right.

An exhilarating benefit of this way of thinking is that full energy can be devoted to current priorities, while knowing other promising possibilities can be addressed in the future.

APPLY

Take a moment to say "Later" to good ideas that need to be set aside now—but which merit future consideration.

"Later" List:

1. _____

2. _____

3. _____

4. _____

5. _____

3. Say "Never" to things of secondary importance

A third way to say "No" is by saying "Never" to things of secondary importance. Some good pursuits will *never* be worth undertaking because they will never be as important as some other things.

An example of this is in how we develop our talent. The Gallup Organization has conducted extensive research on talent.

Their conclusion: we all have it. However, instead of focusing on cultivating our talents, we often waste energy shoring up our weaknesses.

Greatness isn't achieved by trying to be better at something we're not naturally good at. Greatness comes from developing our most valuable talents.

Management guru Peter Drucker said, "The great mystery isn't that people do things badly but that they occasionally do a few things well... Strength is always specific. Nobody ever commented, for example, that the great violinist Jascha Heifetz probably couldn't play the trumpet very well."[2]

Does it matter that Tiger Woods doesn't excel at the piano?

Or that Julia Roberts isn't a renowned chef?

Or that Steve Jobs has never won an Academy Award?

These men and women disciplined themselves to say "Never" to things of secondary importance to them.

Jim Collins says, "Everyone would like to be the best, but most... lack the discipline to figure out with egoless clarity what they *can*

> "Things which matter most must never be at the mercy of things which matter least."
> Goethe, German writer

be the best at and the will to do whatever it takes to turn that potential into reality... It takes discipline to say "No, thank you," to big opportunities. The fact that something is 'a once-in-a-lifetime opportunity' is irrelevant if it doesn't fit..."[3]

Our talents, opportunities, and priorities are like gems. Many "gems" of varying quality are available to us. Saying "Never" involves recognizing the varying quality of these gems, and setting aside the lesser gems to polish the *diamonds*.

APPLY

Take a few moments to say, "Never" to some "lesser gems" that have been—and always will be—of secondary importance to you. Create time and space that enables you to invest more time polishing your diamond-quality talents, opurtunities, and priorties.

"Never" List:

1. _____

2. _____

3. _____

4. _____

5. _____

Say "No" now

Lee Iacocca, former Chairman of Chrysler, said, "If you want to make good use of your time, you've got to know what's most important and then give it all you've got." By saying "No" you will increase the impact of your efforts. Say "No" today so you can say "Yes" to your most important priorities.

QUICK TIP FOR SALES PROFESSIONALS

Say "No" to your least attractive opportunities.

Identify one client, prospect, and opportunity that you should say "No" to so you have more time to invest in more valuable opportunities.

CLIENT _____

PROSPECT _____

OPPORTUNITY _____

Stick With It

ACT
Do something now

"The longest journey starts with just one step."

Tao Te Ching

Do something now—I mean literally, right now!

One of the great—and simplest—strategies to overcome distraction is to *do something right now* that moves us toward the goal.

For example,

- If you're working on a weight-loss goal and in line at Starbucks, order a drink one size smaller.
- If working on a sales goal, put this book down and call that important customer.
- If working on a personal growth goal, go online and order a book that has been highly recommended.

Why act now?

Acting now strengthens our "action muscle." It makes further action easier. It gets a person moving in the direction of his or her goals.

Centuries ago, the Tartar tribes of Asia spoke a curse against their enemies. Their curse was unusual. They didn't say, "May your swords rust in their sheaths," or "May your people be infested with

> *"There is nothing brilliant or outstanding in my record, except perhaps this one thing: I do the things that I believe ought to be done… And when I make up my mind to do a thing, I act."*
> Theodore Roosevelt

pestilence." Instead, their curse was simply, "May you stay in one place forever." *Acting now prevents someone from being stuck in one place forever. It assures forward movement.*

1. Acting now makes us better tomorrow

One of the great benefits of acting now is that it makes someone better tomorrow. This is an irony, because for many of us, one of our great hesitations about acting now is our fear of not doing it right. Perfectionism keeps us from acting and yet it is only through acting that we can perfect our efforts.

A story about an art class illustrates this well. On the first day of class an art teacher told his students, "We're going to work on pottery throughout the semester. I'm going to divide you into two groups and you will work as two teams throughout the semester."

He turned to the right half of the class and said, "You are a group. I want you to focus on *quality*. Your goal is to create a piece of pottery of very high quality. At the end of the semester you will be graded on the pot's *quality*."

Then he turned to his left. "You will also work as a group. But you will be graded on *quantity* not on quality. Make as many pots as you can."

The two groups went to work. The quality group began by studying pottery. They invested weeks analyzing, discussing, and determining exactly what they would build. Finally, they crafted their piece.

The second group approached their work quite differently. They immediately gathered their materials and equipment, got their hands dirty, and from day one started making pots. As they did, they kept learning about pottery and applying the new information to future pieces. By the end of the semester, the second group had produced more than fifty pots. These pots varied in quality, from very poor, which they produced at the beginning of the semester, to quite good, by the end of the semester.

The fascinating result was that the final pot made by the "q u a n t i t y" group was superior in quality to the

> *"The way to succeed is to double your failure rate."*
> Thomas Watson, Founder of IBM

single pot made by the *"quality"* group. The class learned that quality only comes through trial, error, and innovation. They learned that it is more important to get busy and learn on the way than to hold out for perfect circumstances and efforts.

If perfectionism is holding you back from taking action, set it aside, knowing that by acting now you will get better tomorrow.

2. Acting now will open unexpected opportunities

By acting now, we have no idea what opportunities will open to us tomorrow. But they will.

Mountain climber Charles Murray wrote, "Until one is committed, there is hesitancy, the chance to draw back, always ineffectiveness. Concerning all acts of initiative and creation, there is an elementary truth, the ignorance of which kills countless ideas and splendid plans; that the moment one definitely commits oneself, then Providence moves too.

"All sorts of things occur to help one that would never have otherwise occurred. A whole stream of events issues from the decision, raising in one's favor all manner of unforeseen incidents and meetings and material assistance, which no man could have dreamed would have come his way."[1]

Steven Spielberg's story is an inspiring example. At 17, Spielberg took a tour of Universal Studios. On the tour he met Chuck Silvers, head of the studio's editorial department. They talked for awhile and Spielberg convinced Silvers that it would be worthwhile to see some of his amateur 8mm films. Silvers gave him a pass to get on the lot the next day. Young Spielberg's films impressed Silvers. Days later, Spielberg borrowed his dad's briefcase and without permission, walked into the studio. All he had in the briefcase was a sandwich and two candy bars. All summer, the teenage Spielberg showed up in his suit and spent time with directors, writers, and editors. He says, "I found an office that was not being used and became a squatter. I went to a camera store, bought some plastic name tiles and put my name in the building directory: STEVEN SPIELBERG, Room 23C."

And we all know the opportunities and achievements that followed!

When we do something today, we have no idea what opportunities will open to us tomorrow—but they will definitely come.

In sales, this is fundamental, yet we need to be reminded of this truth. Regarding sales calls, my friend Dwayne French says, "While you're sitting around waiting to call, someone else is calling." Jeffrey Fox says in *The Rainmaker,* "The Rainmaker knows one reality: If he doesn't make the selling attempt, there will be no sale."[2] Only by acting today can unexpected opportunities open to us tomorrow.

QUICK TIP FOR SALES PROFESSIONALS

Call now.

Always remember that while you're sitting around waiting to call, someone else is calling. What client or prospect should you call *right now*?

CLIENT/PROSPECT _____

---

3. Acting now creates momentum

Aviator Amelia Earhart said, "The most difficult thing is the decision to act, the rest is merely tenacity. The fears are paper tigers. You can do anything you decide to do. You can act to change and control your life."

We often wait for *motivation* to act, but it usually doesn't come. Motivation usually comes *afterward.* When we take action in the direction of our goal, it often makes us feel great and wanting to take more action.

This is why early Monday morning sales appointments are so valuable for we who sell. Isn't it amazing how we can begin Monday morning sales calls flat-footed from the weekend, only to become completely energized and ready to tackle our week because the call went fabulously well?

Acting now creates momentum and makes it easier to act tomorrow.

> *"We gain strength, courage, and confidence by each experience in which we really stop to look fear in the face... we must do that which we think we cannot."*
>
> Eleanor Roosevelt, First Lady and Diplomat

APPLY: So do it now!

Mark Twain said, "The secret to getting *ahead* is getting started." And entrepreneur Guy Kawasaki added, "The hardest thing about getting *started* is getting started."

My encouragement to you is simple: "Get started!" Don't worry about getting it right. Strengthen the action muscle by taking action now.

Orison Swett Marden believes, "There are two essential requirements for success. The first is 'get-to-it-iveness,' and the second is 'stick-to-it-iveness.' There is no failure for the man who realizes his power, who never knows when he is beaten; there is no failure for the determined endeavor; the unconquerable will. There is no failure for the man who gets up every time he falls, who rebounds like a rubber ball, who persists when everyone else gives up, who pushes on when everyone else turns back."

So, select your top goal.

Now identify one action that you can take *right now* and do it.

Feel good about that action. Don't worry about it not being everything that could be done. Feel good because you took action and you strengthened the action muscle.

My goal:

_____

_____

An action I will take right now:

_____

_____

"Decisiveness is our greatest ally as we chart our path through life. Procrastination is a thief, waiting in disguise to rob us of our hopes and dreams."
Jack Canfield and Mark Victor-Hansen

Stick With It

NOW
Stay in the "now"

5

"One today is worth two tomorrows; what I am to be, I am now becoming."

Benjamin Franklin

The distraction of the past and future
One recurring distraction that slows progress is the past and the future. For example:

- We envision a new result. We get excited about it. Suddenly images of past results flood our mind. We think to ourselves, "I can't accomplish that. Look at how I've done before. If I could accomplish that, I would have already done it."

- We make forward progress toward our goal; then we make a mistake. Suddenly, feelings of failure flood our mind and we question the progress we've made. "Maybe I *can't* do this," we ruminate.

- An unexpected obstacle emerges. Our mind races

toward the future. We start constructing visions of the future that are *not* in line with our desired objectives. Those feelings weigh us down.

Isn't it amazing how we can find ourselves "out of sync," when just days before we were "in the flow" and moving forward? When this happens, the usual culprits are regrets of the past or worries about the future that steal the inspiration that comes from living in the now. The strategy to overcome these distractions is to *stay in the present moment.*

In control or out of control?
When "in the present moment," there is a feeling of control. We recognize the potential of the moment and the ability to make a difference *right now*.

When someone gets "out of the present moment," there is an immediate loss of control. This causes questioning about whether current decisions make any difference at all. Focus disappears and enthusiasm evaporates.

How to stay in the present moment

Tennis legend Jimmy Connors said that during a match, he would only think about the point he was in. He avoided thinking about the game's potential outcome. Instead, he sharpened his energy toward what needed to be done next. When he finished a point, he let it go and became fully absorbed in the next point. [1]

Such an approach is certainly unusual. How can *we* do that? How can *we* stay in the present moment?

1. Process the PAST

When the past crowds in and distracts us, we can't ignore it. The past is a pushy and obnoxious visitor. It won't go away until we process it.

When we lose a point in a tennis match, negative thoughts and emotions *will* flood our minds. We must process them.

When we make a mistake on our diet, negative thoughts and emotions *will* flood our mind. We must process them.

When we are on a sales call and suddenly feel "in over our heads," negative thoughts and emotions *will* flood our mind. We must process them.

How do we process the past?

Forgive it. The first part of processing the past is *forgiving the mistake.* It is essential that we realize that failure is part of the growth process. We can't drag around the baggage of guilt.

Learn from it. Learning from the past makes us better. It also informs our mind that we are *benefiting from the mistake* and this helps our mind process it.

Forget it. When we've accepted that "mistakes are normal" and we've learned from them, we can—and need to—let it go.

We need to drop it and move on to the next moment.

QUICK TIP FOR SALES PROFESSIONALS

Process the past.

What is the single biggest disappointment from the past (whether it happened today or ten years ago), that still keeps you from your very best performance today? How can you learn from past disappointment? When will you fully process it and move on?

_____

_____

---

2. Stop and savor the PRESENT MOMENT

It's easy to miss the beauty and potential of the present moment. French mathematician and philosopher Blaise Pascal powerfully explained how easily we do this:

"We never keep to the present. We recall the past; we anticipate the future as if we found it too slow in coming and were trying to hurry it up, or we recall the past as if to stay its too rapid flight. We are so unwise that we wander about in times that do not belong to us, and do not think of the only one that does; so vain that we dream of times that are not and blindly flee the only one that is. The fact is that the present usually hurts. We thrust it out of sight because it distresses us, and if we find it enjoyable, we are sorry to see it slip away...

"Let each of us examine his thoughts; he will find them wholly concerned with the past or the future. We almost never think of the present, and if we do think of it, it is only to see what light it throws on our plans for the future. The present is never our end.

The past and the present are our means, the future alone our end. Thus we never actually live, but hope to live, and since we are always planning how to be happy, it is inevitable that we should never be so." [2]

Nobel Prize winning scientist Daniel Kahneman says that we experience approximately 20,000 individual moments in a waking day. [3] Stop for a moment and think about that; *twenty-thousand individual moments*. How many of those moments do we *miss* because we are stuck in a *different one?*

> *You've got to get yourself together*
> *You've got stuck in a moment and now you can't get out of it*
> *Don't say that later will be better, now you're stuck in a moment*
> *And you can't get out of it*
> From "Stuck In a Moment You Can't Get Out Of"
> Irish Rock Group, U2

I had a life-changing experience one evening while I was tucking my children into bed. We were working through our bed-time ritual that included brushing teeth, reading stories, saying prayers, sharing hugs, and very bad singing. That evening, like so many others, I was in a hurry to get it all done. This way I could escape downstairs and enjoy a few minutes alone with my wife.

Life was stressful, as it is for all parents of young children. Between work and kids, the pace seemed non-stop until the kids were asleep. That night, like many nights, I rushed through the ritual. Even if my kids didn't realize it, internally, I wanted to get it over with.

But that night, a thought overwhelmed me like five gallons of ice water being poured over a winning football coach: "My six-year-old daughter is one-third of the way out of our home."

The thought stopped me cold.

I looked at her and paused. It seemed like yesterday that we brought her home from the hospital. Now she was *a third of the way out of our house.*

That realization six years ago changed me for good. Now Moriah is *two-thirds* of the way out of the house. With both of our children, I've slowed down and savored the precious moments we have together. When my son David says, as he still does every night, "One more hug," I've got all the time in the world. Why? Because he won't be asking for one more hug much longer. *Now* is the time

> *"It's time to break through the illusion that the best year of your life exists somewhere out there, in the future, when the reality is that it exists right here and now."*
> Debbie Ford

for me to savor these fleeting moments with my children. My encouragement to you is this: stop, claim, and savor *your* present moments.

APPLY: Process the past

Do you need to process something from the past? Is something nagging at you that you need to deal with and put behind you so you can get into the present moment?

If so, take a few minutes right now to process the past.

What specifically do I need to process?

_____

_____

Why can I FORGIVE it?

_____

_____

How can I LEARN from it?

_____

_____

APPLY: Savor the present moment

What are you doing right now? Sipping on a latte? Sitting in a comfortable chair?

Who is around you?

Take a moment to enjoy your latte. Breathe in the moment. Appreciate the people in your life. Recognize even small forward progress toward your goal. Squeeze a little more juice out of this present moment.

Stick With It

SELF-COMPETE
Compete with yourself

6

"Even winning can become routine. Striving ceaselessly to get better and better—and doing it—never becomes routine."

Coach John Wooden

The distraction of others

One of the great distractions in life happens when we get focused on others, rather than staying focused on our goals.

> *"I think I've cared less about 'how can I be more like XXXX' than about just trying to do what I think is fun, interesting, and right. Motto in life: 'Do unto others what you would like others to do unto you. And have fun doing it.'"*
>
> Linus Torvalds, founder of Linux

Think about a sprinter who, as she approaches the finish line, looks to the side to see how she compares with her opponents. Of course, this is deadly!

It's the same with us. Whether the comparison is with those who are underperforming or outperforming us, it detracts from our best performance.

When we compare ourselves to people behind us, we get comfortable, smug, and even arrogant. And we stop pushing.

When we compare ourselves to people ahead of us, we get discouraged and we slow down.

Either way, we will not perform at the highest levels of which we're capable. The strategy to overcome this distraction is simple: *compete against ourselves.*

The story and example of John Wooden

Coach John Wooden is one of the great college coaches of the 20th century. He led the UCLA men's basketball team to ten NCAA championships in 12 seasons.

He's the only man elected to college basketball's Hall of Fame both as a coach and as a player.

As a coach, he was known to the nation for his many championships. To his players, including all-time greats like Kareem Abdul-Jabbar and Bill Walton, he was much more. He was a life mentor.

Said Walton about his coach: "Now I'm forty-four years old and I'm telling my four teenage sons what Coach Wooden used to tell his players. I'm even writing his maxims on their lunch bags and then listening to them complain about it, just like I used to complain. They'll see. My kids will learn. Soon enough they'll come to understand and appreciate the great wisdom of a very wise man: Coach John Wooden."[1]

He didn't talk about winning

One of the most unusual characteristics of Wooden's coaching style was that he did not talk about winning. He felt that an undue focus on a game's outcome ultimately detracted from performance because his players couldn't control the final score. Instead, Wooden taught his players to focus fully on what *was* under their control: their own improvement and performance.

"John Wooden taught us how to focus on one primary objective: be the best you can be in *whatever* endeavor you undertake. Don't worry about the score… Don't worry about the opponent. It sounds easy, but it's actually very difficult." [2]

This principle was forged in the character of John Wooden by watching his father's example during the Great Depression. Despite doing everything he could, his father Joshua Wooden suffered great loss during the Depression. Yet he maintained a balanced perspective. He avoided being devastated and accepted that he could only handle things that were under his control.

This shaped a young John Wooden. It enabled him to navigate through life by focusing on making the most of the situations under his control, while not worrying about the factors that weren't.

How competing with ourselves helps us

When we choose to compete only with ourselves, how does this improve our performance?

> *"People fail for any number of reasons. They may get overwhelmed, feeling that they're in over their head, and lose self-confidence. They may think they've arrived and decide they can relax."*
> Larry Bossidy and Ram Charan,
> in Confronting Reality

1. When we're ahead, it prevents us from becoming *lax*

John Wooden said, "Even winning can become routine. Striving ceaselessly to get better and better—and doing it—never becomes routine."

It's important to remember that comparing ourselves to others is irrelevant. If I can bench-press more than my grandmother, does that make me strong? Does it make her weak? It's an irrelevant comparison.

The only comparison that matters is this: *how much am I living up to my current potential?*

2. When we're behind, it helps us avoid *dicouragement*

The GoalsGuy, Gary Ryan Blair, encourages us to "beware of the *Snow White* trap: the wicked witch can never be happy as long as she continued to compare herself to someone else."[3]

This is a big deal for some people.

Think about your goal. And be honest with yourself. Is there someone you are comparing yourself to, who:

- Is already there?
- Got there sooner?
- Didn't have to work as hard to get there?
- Had an opportunity that you didn't have?

When comparisons to other people are fully realized they can begin to be eliminated, focus on goals can rematerialize, and life can move forward.

3. Today, it helps us put in our *best performance*

Competing with ourselves helps us give our best performance today. Reaching the highest level of potential requires putting in high performance day after day. When people simply focus on becoming their best—rather than comparing themselves with others—they are freed to put in their best performance *today.*

Coach Wooden built sustained success by helping his players work every day to *make each practice a masterpiece.*

Says Wooden, "When I was teaching basketball, I urged my players to try their hardest to improve that very day, to make that practice a masterpiece.

"Too often we get distracted by what is outside our control. You can't do anything about yesterday. The door to the past has been shut and the key thrown away. You can do nothing about tomorrow. It is yet to come. However, tomorrow is in large part determined by what you do today. So make today a masterpiece. You have control over that.

"This rule is even more important in life than basketball. You have to apply yourself each day to become a little better. By applying yourself to the task of becoming a little better each and every day over a period of time, you will become a *lot* better. Only then will you be able to approach being the best you can be."[4]

QUICK TIP FOR SALES PROFESSIONALS

Make today a masterpiece.

What is one way you can improve your game today?

_____

_____

APPLY: Put in a better performance today

Set aside comparisons with others. Remember that what is under your control is *what you do today*. Make today a masterpiece.

Take a moment to identify one way to improve your performance today. And go for it.

> What is one way I can improve my performance today?
>
> _____
>
> _____
>
> _____
>
> _____

ENVIRONMENT
Build an environment that supports you

"Creating a positive environment may lead to success even if a person is not fully motivated, because positive environments help the person retain good habits."

Farrokh Alemi, PhD, Journal of Healthcare Quality

Environment influences our choices more than we realize

Because people ultimately make their own decisions, they are largely unaware of the *influence* environment has on the decisions they make.

In the bestselling book, *The Tipping Point,* Malcolm Gladwell shared a study about the role environmental factors played on the decision-making of a group of seminary students.

The study sought to identify factors influencing student decisions to stop and help a person in need. The students, unaware of the study, were instructed to prepare a presentation on helping people in need. They were then sent to a different location to give their presentations. The alleyway they took for the presentation required them to, quite literally, step over a person in need.

Amazingly, many of the students didn't stop. Even though they had devoted their studies to helping people in need and were engaged in teaching on the topic, many didn't actually do it. In fact, only one factor made a big difference in the study results, and that was *time*. The perception on the part of the students about how much time they had was the only factor that influenced whether or not they stopped. Students who were told they were running late and needed to hurry passed over the person in need. Students who were told they had extra time were much more likely to stop. *All the good intentions in the world didn't impact their decision to act as much as the environmental factor of how much time they had.*[1]

Two ways to gain—or lose—35 pounds

To gain 35 pounds for the movie *Syriana*, actor George Clooney intentionally ate six daily meals to gain one pound every day.

That's one way to gain 35 pounds.

The other way is simpler. Work in a bakery.

If we have a sweet tooth, the weight magically begins to appear. Without strategy, plan, or intentional focus, weight gain comes easily.

I recently asked a woman who owned a bakery how she kept the weight off when she bought the bakery; her reply was, "I didn't. Within a couple months I

> *Our choice of a "reference group"—the people that we regularly associate with—is the most important determiner of our results.*
> Dr. David McClelland, Harvard University

50

gained 23 pounds. And then my doctor said I needed to get control of it." Now she is fighting against the continual bombardment of messages and temptations from her environment.

Likewise, to *lose 35* pounds, someone can create a detailed plan *or* simply get into an environment that supports weight loss. Joining a group like Weight Watchers or PeerTrainer.com leads to a cascading of choices that result in weight loss.

Three ways to improve our environment

We shape our environment—and then our environment shapes us. Environmental improvements make ongoing decisions easier. Here are three different ways to improve environment.

1. INPUT: Feed your mind healthy food

The first way to improve environment is to improve what we is put into the mind.

Charlie "Tremendous" Jones says, "You will be in five years where you are today except for the people you meet and the books you read."

What you read and listen to will plant new ideas, stir creativity, and reinforce a "can-do" attitude.

Or, what you read and listen to can discourage creativity and create a pessimistic, negative worldview.

I cut my teeth selling by listening to motivational expert, Zig Ziglar, in my car. After months of selling, I noticed a substantial swing in production from month to month. I also observed a relationship between what I listened to while I was driving and my sales production.

So I made an intentional study. I discovered that when I

listened to audio material on sales and motivation, my sales were significantly higher than if I listened to news and talk radio.

Since I've shared that story in training sessions, other sales professionals have chosen to conduct the experiment and found similar results. When we listen to material that stirs creativity and encourages us, we get "on our game," and perform at a higher level.

> *"Never curse commuting time. Simply find a way to let it work for you."*
> Ted Schwartz,
> Time Management for Writers

The same is true in other arenas as well.

If working on a financial, relational, or health goal, listening to encouraging and insightful material "on topic" will likewise improve performance. It is an important way to improve the personal environment.

2. REMINDERS: Surround yourself with reminders

A second way to improve our environment is to surround ourselves with reminders.

As Gary Ryan Blair says, "A decision to achieve a goal is never made just once, it happens continuously. A goal requires a focused commitment of energy."[2]

This is where reminders help. They keep goals in the forefront. They keep nudging people in the direction of the goal.

Reminders can be as simple as having periodicals and books in easy-to-access places, like on a nightstand and in the bathroom, where they will be picked up from time to time.

Reminders can be as simple as placing a priority list on the door.

In *Organized For Success*, Stephanie Winston describes the

daily habit of Norman Rentrop, CEO of the German publishing house Rentrop Verlag. Rentrop posts his top priority item on a sign on the inside of his office door. When he hangs his coat first thing in the morning, the sign asks him, "What will I do today to reach this goal?" Then at the end of the day as he grabs his coat, it likewise asks, "What have I done today to accomplish this goal?" [3]

The beauty of simple reminders is that they nudge us in the direction of our goals.

3. PEOPLE: Spend time with people who lift you

A third way to improve environment is by spending more time with people who lift and encourage.

People are a huge part of our environment. We affect the behavior of people around us and they affect us.

Every parent knows this. Children pick up the mannerisms, attitudes, perspectives, and behaviors of their peers. Parents, therefore, are very concerned about who their children spend time with.

We don't grow out of this. Fascinating research has been conducted that illustrates how our brains work on a subconscious level to mimic behaviors of those with whom we're interacting. [4]

It appears that we are "wired" to connect. We look for common ground and take on the characteristics of one another. Overall, this is a great thing. But when we recognize the immense influence people have on each other, it is wise to consider spending more time with people who increase performance by modeling successful behavior.

Orison Swett Marden said, "Your outlook upon life, your estimate of yourself, your estimate of your value, are largely colored by your environment. Your whole career will be modified, shaped, molded by your surroundings, by the character of the people with whom you come in contact every day."

There are four types of people who inhabit the success environment: Models, Fellow Travelers, Team Members and Cheerleaders. All of these people are invaluable and can be discovered by asking these questions:

- Who is *currently where I want to be*? These people are the Models. They provide insight and the continual reminder that *achieving worthwhile goals is possible*.

- Who is *going where I want to go*? These people are the Fellow Travelers. As in cycling, we "draft" one another, gaining speed because we have the same destination.

- Who can *help me get where I am going*? These people are valuable Team Members. They have information or connections that can help us.

- Who *genuinely wants me to get there*? These people are the Cheerleaders. They encourage, inspire, and keep us going. As Zig Ziglar says, "Encouragement is oxygen to the soul." Cheerleaders keep the oxygen supply full.

> *9 of 10 people say they are more productive when around positive people.*[5]

APPLY: How strong is your team?

As you look over the four kinds of people in your environment, ask yourself, *how strong is my team?* Take a few minutes to think about your team members.

* Who are my Models?

_____

* Who are my Fellow Travelers?

_____

* Who are my Team Members?

_____

* Who are my Cheerleaders?

_____

APPLY: Improve your team

After considering the four questions, where do you need help? Who can you add to your team? Will this mean joining a group, initiating a new relationship, or becoming more intentional about time with particular people? Take a few minutes to improve your team.

* Do I need more Models? If so, who?

_____

* Do I need more Fellow Travelers? If so, who?

_____

* Do I need more Team Members? If so, who?

_____

* Do I need more Cheerleaders? If so, who?

_____

QUICK TIP FOR SALES PROFESSIONALS

Get around people who are passionate about selling.

Who do you spend time with that is _passionate_ about selling? Who _should_ you spend more time with?

_____

_____

_____

_____

Part 2

OVERCOMING INERTIA

Most of a rocket's fuel is used up in the first few minutes of flight. So it is in reaching goals. To achieve new results, the inertia of old behaviors, attitudes, and patterns must be overcome. It takes a lot of energy to break through inertia. The second seven strategies provide fuel for the journey.

Stick With It

PURPOSE
Anchor your goals to deeper purpose

"Purpose creates a destination."

Jim Loehr and Tony Schwartz

Reasons are rocket fuel

Most of a rocket's fuel is used up in the first minutes of its journey into space. *The reasons why* people want to reach their goals can be likened to that explosive fuel. Without good reasons, no one can break out of the gravity of old attitudes, behaviors and patterns.

Think about the Apollo Missions. Years of engineering prowess and collaboration were required to design a craft that could transport human beings to the moon. But without fuel, the ship would have remained on the landing pad.

"Our goals can only be reached through a vehicle of a plan, in which we must fervently believe, and upon which we must vigorously act. There is no other route to success."
Pablo Picasso

Many good goals never get off the launch pad for lack of fuel. There just aren't compelling reasons to keep working toward their fulfillment.

Pushing out of the comfort zone

A comfort zone is an immense gravitational force in someone's life. It is far easier to act within a comfort zone than to move outside. There must be compelling reasons to venture out.

Powerful purpose supplies those reasons.

As authors Jim Lohr and Tony Schwartz have written, "Purpose is what lights us up, floats our boats, feeds our souls."

Three places to anchor our goals

Vince Lombardi, Jr. says, "A goal without a purpose is like a boat without an anchor." Here are three places that can provide strong anchorage for goals.

1. A passion for the work itself

One of the places to anchor goals is in a passion for the work itself. When an enduring passion for the work is present, so, too, is the likelihood of achieving the stated goal.

Award-winning director Francis Ford Coppola said, "Passions are wired into the real world more directly than our workday routines are. If you love something, you'll bring so much of yourself to it that it will create your future."

> "The secret of success is making your vocation your vacation."
> Mark Twain

This can't be overstated. In the book, *Good to Great*, Jim Collins points out, "Those who turn good into great are motivated by a deep *creative urge* and an *inner compulsion* for sheer unadulterated excellence *for its own sake.* Those who build and perpetuate mediocrity, in contrast, are motivated more by the fear of being left behind." [1]

Howard Schultz, architect of the Starbucks brand, exemplifies this type of passion. Says Schultz, "Everything we do matters." Dub Hay, Starbucks' Senior Vice President for coffee and global procurement, showed him a bag of rare Ethiopian beans. A statement on the bag caught Schultz's eyes. It said the bean had an "intense blueberry flavor," to which Schultz strongly objected, concerned that customers might think the blueberry was added. Although Hay and the team convinced Schultz to keep the phrase, he recalled, "Three words on a bag. Howard just cares so incredibly much what we put out." [2] That kind of passion motivates a leader like Howard Schultz to take action day after day in a way that builds his company.

> *"Everyone should carefully observe which way his heart draws him, and then choose that way with all his strength."*
> Hasidic saying

Likewise, when our goal is anchored to a passion for the work itself, it inspires us day after day.

Get more passionate about the work itself

To stir our passion, we may need to *restate our goal.* Sometimes a slight goal adjustment puts our goal into the "sweet spot" of current passions. For example, a weight loss goal may have focused on dietary changes, when it might be easier to tap into a latent passion for activity and exercise.

Or, to stir passion, we may need to *totally immerse ourselves* in the goal. Most people who achieve new goals become aficionados of the new area they have embraced. By becoming immersed in the literature and culture of the new arena, passion is stirred.

Or, to stir passion we may need to *maintain a strict focus* on the elements that inspire us. This focus keeps passion burning when the unpleasantries arrive. For example, few sales people enjoy "cold calling." Top producers look beyond the parts of their sales careers that are unpleasant and keep passion stirred by focusing on the parts they love, like closing business.

By tying goals into a passion for the work itself, it becomes easier to work toward them on a daily basis.

2. A vision of ourselves at our best

A second place to anchor goals is in the mind. Each person should envision themselves at their best.

Pat Murray says, "If you want to see someone in real pain, watch someone who knows who he is and defaults on it on a regular basis."[3]

A twenty-something Jim Rohn was told by his mentor, Mr. Schof, "Set a goal to become a millionaire." Says Rohn, "I liked the sound of that: *millionaire.*" Then Mr. Schof asked Jim if he knew *why* he should set that goal. Rohn thought to himself, "I can think of a *lot* of reasons." But Mr. Schof told him, "No. Set a goal to become a millionaire because of *what it will make of you to achieve it.*"

This may be the greatest benefit of setting and achieving goals; *what we become in the process of achieving them.*

> *"Cancer taught me a plan for more purposeful living, and that in turn taught me how to train and to win more purposefully.*
> *It taught me that pain has a reason, and that sometimes the experience of losing things… has its own value in the scheme of life.*
> *Pain and loss are great enhancers."*
> Lance Armstrong

APPLY: What will my goal require me to become?

What will your goal require you to become? Does it help you tap into your highest potential? If not, may I suggest that you adjust your goal to tap into a vision of yourself at your best?

Take a few minutes to think about your goal. Then think about *what it will require you to become in order to achieve it.*

My goal and what it will require me to become

My goal: _____

What will it require me to become in order to achieve it?

_____

_____

_____

---

3. An impact greater than our happiness

A third place to anchor goals is in their impact being greater than our personal happiness.

We've grown up in a self-indulgent period. The reasons for setting and achieving goals are often anchored in self-indulgence.

> *"The unexamined life is not worth living."*
> Socrates
>
> *"There's got to be more to life than being really, really, really ridiculously good-looking."*
> Derek Zoolander, silver-screen male model and philosopher

For example, goals involving increased sales may involve the carrot of personal wish lists of things a person wants to buy or exotic places they want to go.

If someone sets a weight-loss goal, they may picture their tanned and toned bodies in the mirror and imagine how much better they'll look.

While these reasons are valuable, legitimate, and often useful, they can come up short. Here's why: they may not be solid enough. They may not "hold."

If my biggest motivator for losing weight is how I will look in the mirror, that "indulgence" may be trumped by the indulgence of a burger.

In regard to sales, many salespeople are comfortable financially. Many of us have nice vehicles, a big-screen TV, an annual tropical vacation, and designer clothes. Why bust our butts for a little more money?

This is where *deeper purpose* takes us to a new level.

Best-selling author Rick Warren writes, "The purpose of your life is far greater than your own personal fulfillment… or even your happiness."

Seeing personal wealth or good health habits as an example to children, influencing them for life, can lift motivation to a whole new level. In the sales arena, if someone chooses to give a percentage of their income to a charitable cause,

> *"Most people can discern the difference between a salesperson who is out to make a dollar and one who is out to make a difference."*
> Todd Duncan

imagine what that can do to passion, focus, and drive. Peter Drucker wrote, "The effective person focuses on contribution. He looks up from his work and outward toward goals. He asks, 'What can I contribute…?'" [4]

QUICK TIP FOR SALES PROFESSIONALS

Make a difference.

What could you do to tie achievement of your current sales goal into making a difference? It could be something as simple as attaching a portion of your sales increase to a charitable cause that matters to you. What could you do that would inject a fresh dose of purpose and passion into your effort?

_____

_____

_____

_____

APPLY: Tie your goal into a contribution and kick things up a notch

Remember, the point here is not to devalue the other motivators that have already stirred us. Instead, it is to *add* to them.

Take a few minutes to think about your goal. Then think about *why* you want to accomplish it.

Consider how you can tie your goal into a contribution greater than your own happiness and kick things up a notch.

My goal and how it will contribute beyond my own happiness

My goal: _____

How will it contribute? _____

_____

FIRE

Fire yourself up by making your goal more compelling

"A fire in the heart lifts everything in your life."

John Maxwell

Compelling goals set us on fire

In 1961, President John F. Kennedy articulated a stirring and ambitious goal to the nation. He promised that by the end of the decade, the United States would place a man on the moon and return him safely to earth. Spoken at the height of the cold war, his words galvanized Congress and the nation and gave rise to the commitment necessary to make the dream a reality.

Imagine how different the result would have been if he had stood up in 1961 and said, "We're going to beef up the space program."[1] To fire up the people and garner the resources necessary, Kennedy had to make the goal powerfully compelling.

One of the important ways to break out of inertia is to make goals more compelling. The goals themselves may be good enough, but they must be stated in a way that moves those involved to take consistant action.

Are you pursuing something *remarkable?*

In *The Magic Lamp,* Keith Ellis writes, "Perhaps the most startling truth about human nature is that anyone can do something truly remarkable in life if he or she has something truly remarkable to do." [2]

We all want to be part of something special. We all want to accomplish remarkable things. Let me ask you a question: do your goals, as stated, give you the sense that you are pursuing something remarkable?

If our goals feel *remarkable* to us, they will fire us up and help us press through discouragement.

How to make our goals more compelling

Practically, how do we do it? How do we polish a good goal and make it more compelling? We do it by making our goals bigger, clearer, and bolder.

1. Make it BIGGER

One of the ways to make a goal more compelling is by making it bigger. In *A Bias For Action,* the authors write, "Goals have an enormously energizing effect on people, particularly when they are clear and well defined, and when they are ambitious enough to be challenging yet not so unrealistic that they're paralyzing." [3]

When Jeff Bezos launched Amazon.com, he didn't seek to merely offer a few more titles than the brick-and-mortar stores. The big bookstores offered 250,000 books. Instead, Bezos offered a staggering *three million* titles through his online store.

Big goals energize us!

Are your goals big enough?

Matching last year's sales growth may not stir you. But doubling that growth might. How about breaking into a whole new level of account? Is your goal big enough to stir your juices?

> *"My goal is simple. It is a complete under-standing of the universe, why it is as it is and why it exists at all."*
> Stephen Hawking, physicist

Isn't it time to feel that passion again?

Sometimes people just need to make the goal bigger.

APPLY: Take the BIGGER test. Is your goal big enough to stir you to take action?

What is my goal?

_____

How well does it stir me to take action?

_____

If it doesn't stir me, how can I restate it so it does?

_____

2. Make it CLEARER

Another way to make a goal more compelling is to make it clearer. A persuasive variety of studies confirm the power of clarity in goal achievement. Jim Lohr and Tony Schwartz capture a number of these studies in *The Power of Full Engagement.*[4]

In one study, participants were asked to write a paper on how they planned to spend Christmas Eve. Half the group was told to specify the exact time and place where they would write the report. The other group was not given a deadline. Nearly 75% of the group with the deadline turned in their reports compared with 33% of the other group.

In another study, the goal was to get more non-exercising college students into a fitness program. Compliance improved from 29% to 39% when students were given information about the benefits of exercise. But the results skyrocketed to 91% when students were asked to identify when and where they intended to exercise.

Clarifying goals *makes them actionable.* Vague goals don't show what's next. *When a goal is clear, it becomes more compelling because it beckons us to take specific action.*

APPLY: Take the CLEARER test. Does your goal beckon you to take specific action?

What is my goal?

_____

What does it compel me to do next?

_____

If it isn't clear, how can I restate it so it is clear enough to compel me to take specific action?

_____

3. Make it BOLDER

Another way to make a goal more compelling is to make it bolder.

Innovation and marketing guru Seth Godin told me, "In our environment, safe is risky and risky is safe."[5]

Today it is more important than ever to set goals that are daring, risky, and bold. Otherwise, they simply will not captivate anyone's attention.

> "Bite off more than you can chew. And then chew it."
>
> Ella Williams

Boldness has characterized the lives and leadership of Google founders Larry Page and Sergey Brin. Their own words sum up the compulsion behind their actions, "We want to be bold—we want to make a big difference."

While making goals bigger is about *size*, making them bolder is about *daring*. Bolder goals require someone to step out more, to put more skin in the game, to risk humiliation. Bold goals make us *sweat*.

I have spoken publicly more than 2,000 times in my career and still get butterflies before presentations. I've come to *value* that. A speech coach told me years ago, "If you get beyond the butterflies, you have become too comfortable." He told me that if I was stretching myself, I would feel butterflies, and they would actually keep me on my toes and help me perform at a higher level. I have found that to be wise advice.

Helen Keller said, "Security is mostly a superstition. It does not exist in nature. Life is either a daring adventure or nothing."

Make sure your goals are bold enough to make you sweat!

APPLY: Take the BOLDER test. Is your goal bold enough to make you sweat?

What is my goal?

_____

Is it bold enough to make me sweat?

_____

If it doesn't, how can I restate it so it is does?

_____

QUICK TIP FOR SALES PROFESSIONALS

Think bigger.

What could you atempt, that if successful, would take your business to a whole new level?

_____

_____

_____

IDEAS

Discover small ideas that can help you improve

"It isn't so much what you know when you start that matters. It's what you learn and put to use after you open your doors that counts most."

Entrepreneur, as quoted by David Schwartz in The Magic of Thinking Big

Ideas as rocket fuel

Ideas fuel growth and progress. Ideas counter the negative feelings that come with feeling stuck. Ideas provide new approaches to old challenges. Ideas turn good strategies into great ones. Lots of small ideas pave the way for achieving big goals.

> *"What's in an idea? Ideas are the engine of progress. They improve people's lives by creating better ways to do things. They build and grow successful organizations and keep them healthy and prosperous."*
> Alan G. Robinson and Dean M. Schroeder in Ideas Are Free

Small ideas can make a big difference

Fifteen years ago, someone suggested I replace the typical burger with a sub sandwich. That one idea has kept five pounds off my frame since.

Last year, I sought a replacement drink for high calorie Frappucinos. I enjoy doing work at Starbucks, but knew I couldn't keep drinking 700 calorie drinks. After some nutritional research, I landed on a replacement drink: a half-chocolate soy mocha. With just 225 calories, moderate sugar, and loaded with soy protein, the drink has been a healthy and easy change.

In sales and marketing, small changes can also make big differences.

Consider the story of sliced bread. The term, "It's the best thing since sliced bread," means something is bound for instant acceptance. But in fact it took *12 years* to catch on. It wasn't until sliced bread was marketed with the message, "Builds strong bodies ten ways" that it took off.

How to become an "idea machine"

While big ideas are more tantalizing, small ideas bring about most sustained improvement. In 1992, Yuzo Yasuda published *40 Years, 20 Million Ideas*, a book about Toyota's "idea system." Toyota gets

> *"More gold has been mined from the thoughts of men than has ever been taken from the earth."*
> Napoleon Hill

better year after year through a relentless approach to continual, incremental improvement. In Japanese business, this approach is called *kaizen*. Toyota has a group in Kentucky called their *Kaizen*

Team which invests itself fully developing new ideas for ongoing, small improvements.

Generating new ideas is important because we don't know which ones will be instrumental in smashing old limitations. But some of them will. Generating new ideas is a useful strategy that accelerates us out of the inertia of old perpectives, patterns, and results.

How do we generate more ideas? How do we, as Brian Tracy says, "become an idea machine?" Here are three ways:

1. Experience new things

One of the ways to generate new ideas is to have new experiences. We easily get stuck in the ruts of going to the same places, spending time with the same people, and reading the same kinds of books. Breaking the mold and experiencing new things is a refreshing and enjoyable way to acquire a whole new perspective and set of ideas.

Here are some practical suggestions:

- Read books, articles, and blogs by people outside your usual interest group.
- Spend time with people who have achieved a goal you would like to achieve, but who have gone about it in a very different way.
- Employ a strategy completely outside your comfort zone.

> *"If we are only willing to behave like all the others, we will see the same things, hear the same things, hire similar people, come up with similar ideas, and develop identical products and services. We will drown in the sea of normalcy."*
> Jonas Ridderstrale and Kjell Nordstom,
> quoted in The Deviant's Advantage

2. Ask new questions

Another way to generate new ideas is to ask new questions.

The Walt Disney Company did this when they redesigned Disneyland's Tomorrowland. Originally, Tomorrowland was built around the view of the future people held in the 1950s. For years, Disney knew that Tomorrowland needed a redesign. They struggled with how those changes would look. The problem was that the popular view of the future had darkened considerably. Rather than the bright and clean view reminiscent of the old Jetson's cartoon, the new view was more in keeping with the 1984 movie *Bladerunner*. That science fiction movie pictured a dark future where technology was more foe than friend. Disney executives could not envision how to create a *Bladerunner*-style Tomorrowland in "the happiest place on earth."

Disney broke the impasse by asking a new question.

> *"We all need an occasional whack on the side of the head to shake us out of routine patterns, to force us to rethink our problems, and to stimulate us to ask new questions that may lead to other right answers."*
> Roger Von Oech in A Whack on the Side of the Head

Tomorrowland had been built in response to the question, "What do people think the future will be?" Disney leaders changed the question. They asked, "What do people *want* the future to be?" They came to the conclusion that people *want* the future to be like Montana. They desire a future where technology helps bring us closer to the environment. Suddenly, Disney had what they needed to rebuild Tomorrowland in a way that matched the overall park.

APPLY: Ask a new question about your old challenge
What *new* question could you ask about your *old* challenge? New

> "When you can do nothing, what can you do?"
> Zen koan

questions lead to new solutions. Take a few moments to generate a new question.

Old challenge:

_____

New question:

_____

3. Capture your ideas
Another way to become an "idea machine" is by capturing more of your ideas. For many, this comes in the form of a journal or "capture book."

Let me ask you this question: have you ever had a great idea come to you in one of these situations?

- While driving?
- Lying in bed?
- Taking a shower?
- Over lunch?
- During a meeting?

The best ideas often come on the fly.

That's why the experts encourage carrying something to capture ideas.

Richard Branson of Virgin Airlines has engaged in this practice for a long time. When he travels on his airline, he makes lists of potential improvements, such as how well the seats recline, or how quickly attendants help wheelchair-bound passengers.

Something as simple as a $10 journal can be a key to capturing ideas that provide a catapult to speedier goal-achievement.

QUICK TIP FOR SALES PROFESSIONALS

Make capturing ideas easier.

The sales profession requires a lot of creativity. How can you make it easier to capture your ideas, no matter where you are?

_____

_____

APPLY: Create a basket of ideas

Generate some ideas. Take a few minutes to brainstorm a dozen ideas that might help you achieve your goal. Do it by answering this question: "What are a dozen ideas that could potentialy help you acheive your goals?"

Remember that the point here is to generate ideas—not select which ones you will act on. Let your creative juices flow and create a basket of ideas!

Basket of ideas
1 _____
2 _____
3 _____
4 _____
5 _____
6 _____
7 _____
8 _____
9 _____
10_____
11_____
12_____

Stick With It

SMALL IMPROVEMENTS
Make small incremental improvements

"Many things which cannot be overcome when they are taken together, yield themselves up when taken little by little."

Plutarch

When enthusiasm sours

Haven't we all been really enthusiastic about something only to end up disappointed in the end? This is a big type of inertia that requires a substantial push to get through.

We begin the year deciding that we're finally going to get in shape and take our health seriously. In January, we eat better, hit the gym, and make exciting progress. By summer, the enthusiasm and progress are a distant memory and we're disappointed that our sincere efforts led nowhere.

We attend a sales seminar and get "psyched up." We get motivated to higher performance, taking the presenter at her word, believing we can take our business to the next level. A week later the daily grind has crowded out the new possibilities and we become cynical about what we experienced.

As a keynote presenter, trainer, and writer, I am *very sensitive* to this. I want you to see the potential of *taking things up a notch on a sustained basis*. I want to help you take the long-term view. Remember that we tend to *over-estimate* what we can accomplish in the *short-term*, but we *under-estimate* what we can accomplish in the *long-term*.

One small improvement at a time

One of the ways to break out of inertia is by getting better *one small improvement at a time.*

> *"The little things. There's nothing bigger, is there?"*
> David Ames, played by Tom Cruise in Vanilla Sky

How small improvements help

Small improvements help in different ways. Let's explore two of the distinct ways small improvements help break through inertia.

1. Small improvements sometimes MAKE A BIG DIFFERENCE

A *single new sales skill* can dramatically improve results. This is especially true in key points of customer interaction, such as leaving voice mail messages, getting the first appointment, handling an objection, or asking for the business.

Making an exercise commitment more convenient can make all the difference. A change as simple as joining a club that is *on our drive path* instead of out of the way can determine whether or not we follow through.

A terrific example of this occurred many years ago when the president of a steel company hired an efficiency expert named Ivy

Lee to suggest ways he could improve his business. Lee provided suggestions and afterward the president said he really didn't need more ideas, because they weren't effectively using the knowledge they already had.

Yet the president gave Lee a chance. He told Lee that if he could show them a way to become more productive, he would pay him anything he asked.

Lee presented the president with one small idea for improvement.

Giving the president a piece of paper, Lee asked him to jot down the most important five or six things he needed to do the next day. The president took a few minutes to do it. Then Lee asked him to list those items in order of their importance.

Finally Lee instructed the president to put the paper in his pocket and pull it out the next day, working on the first item until completed. After that he was to move to the second, then the third, and so on. He didn't have to worry about completing each of them because he would have taken care of his most important priorities already.

Finally Lee told the president to do this for a number of days and then push the practice out to his managers.

Instead of charging a fee, Lee simply asked the president to send him a check for whatever he felt the idea was worth. A few weeks later, the president sent Ivy Lee a check for $25,000, saying it was the most profitable idea he had ever received.[1]

See the *big* potential of the *small* improvement!
Don't minimize the big potential of small improvements. Every small improvement has big potential.

Coach John Wooden taught this to his teams every season.

During the first day of practice, Coach Wooden would personally show his players how to properly put on their sweat socks. Few coaches would ever teach something so basic. But the coach reasoned, "An improperly worn sock could lead to a blister. A blister leads to pain. Pain leads to distraction. Distraction can lead to a turnover. A turnover could lose the game. *And the game could be the national championship.*"

In basketball, small improvements—like properly worn sweat socks—can make a big difference.

So it is for us. There is big potential in small improvements.

QUICK TIP FOR SALES PROFESSIONALS

Make sure you have a great reason every time you call your clients.

What is one way you can make your clients more excited about taking your call?

_____

_____

---

2. Small improvements always COMPOUND

Another way small improvements help is by compounding. The compounding gains of small changes are not readily obvious, so small changes may not be as attractive as big changes. However, compounding adds up over the long-term.

Reducing calorie intake just 100 calories per day will result in losing one pound every month and 12 pounds over the course of a year. A dozen pounds can be shed half a candy bar at a time.

Making one more new prospect call at the end of every day will generate 200 new opportunities over the course of a year. What might that do to your sales numbers?

Increasing a loyal customer base by a few percentage points can dramatically improve profitability. Southwest Airlines, the perpetual profit-machine of the airline industry, has a *highly engaged customer base of only 27%.* But the 22 percentage points that separate it from a competitor like United Airlines, at 5%, is enormous. [2]

Listening to insightful and inspiring audio material during part of the commute can easily provide one new idea daily, totaling 20 new ideas every month. If one or two of those ideas were put into practice every month, how might that help in reaching goals?

In *Ideas Are Free*, the authors tell a story about one small improvement that greatly helped John D. Rockefeller's Standard Oil. In the 1870s, Rockefeller visited a Long Island refinery. While inspecting a production line where kerosene was being put into containers for export, he asked a worker how many drops of solder was used to seal the container lids. The answer, "Forty." Rockefeller asked if he could do it with thirty-eight. Although that wasn't feasible, the team was able to reduce the number of drops to *thirty-nine.*

In retirement, Rockefeller reflected on the compounding effect of this small improvement: "That one drop of solder saved $2,500 the first year; but the export business... became immensely greater than it was then; and

> *"It takes 1%. Top performers aren't 100% better in any one area… They're 1% better in hundreds of areas."*
> Thomas A Freese

the saving has gone steadily along, one drop on each can, and has amounted since to many hundreds of thousands of dollars."[3]

APPLY: Make a small, sustainable change

As small changes are made, it's important to be pragmatic and make sure they're sustainable. We must be able to live with the changes.

My friend Charles Platkin is a nutrition expert and author. His books and online coaching business have helped tens of thousands of people make sustainable health changes. Charles says that if people want to sustain changes, they need to make adjustments that can be lived with for the rest of that person's life.

And he models sustainable change.

While staying in his home, he introduced me to *I Can't Believe It's Not Butter* spray, some outstanding diet soda, and healthy ways to make potatoes that actually taste good. It was refreshing not to have him go into a diatribe about aspartame, hidden chemicals, or everything that's bad about potatoes. Charles eats and lives healthfully and *sustainably*. He can live with his changes. And he helps scores of others because his encouragement is pragmatic.[4]

We need to take the same approach to *our* changes. We need to be realistic about the changes we're making. They need to stretch us but we need to be able to sustain them for the long haul.

Take a few minutes now to examine one change you are making and be pragmatic. If you need to, refine it so it is sustainable over the long term.

The change:

_____

How sustainable is it?

_____

Why?

_____

If it isn't, how can I adjust it to make it sustainable long-term?

_____

_____

Stick With It

MOMENTUM

Turn your wins into winning streaks

"Streaks start to run on their own momentum, producing conditions that make further success or failure more likely. Winning creates a positive aura around everything…. In short, confidence grows in winning streaks and helps propel a tradition of success."

Rosabeth Moss Kanter, Harvard Business School

Negative and positive momentum

Momentum is a powerful force. Negative momentum is one type of inertia that must be overcome in the pursuit of goals.

Rosabeth Moss Kanter, who has made the study of momentum in business and sport a specialty, says, "On the way up, success creates positive momentum. People who believe they are likely to win are also likely to put in the extra effort at difficult moments to ensure that victory. On the way down, failure feeds on itself. As performance starts running on a positive or negative path, momentum can be hard to stop. Growth cycles produce optimism, decline cycles produce pessimism."[1]

One of the ways to make this work is by protecting wins jealously and being sure they're being extended into winning streaks.

Making momentum work for us

Just as negative momentum from past results can result in pessimism, positive momentum can be turned into winning streaks and put to work.

Brian Tracy applies Sir Isaac Newton's famous words to human momentum, "A person in motion tends to remain in

> *"The harder you work the harder it is to surrender."*
> Vince Lombardi

motion; it takes much less energy to keep moving than it does to stop and try to start moving again."[2]

How to turn our wins into winning streaks

1. Value momentum

To turn our wins into winning streaks, we must value momentum. Best-selling author Spencer Johnson makes the point that completing a task or project, even if small, seems to "build energy and confidence to succeed in the next task."

If we're not careful, we can fritter away our gains. It's like Keith

> *"It's a very simple dynamic that you're working under. Losing begets losing, winning begets winning. Players want to be on winning teams. They want to be champions. So as you win, things come together."*
> Chris Wallace, general manager, Boston Celtics

Ellis says, "Sometimes when you're nearing the end of a long and demanding wish, you feel an almost irresistible urge to let down, to relax. Resist it. It's like that warm, cozy feeling you get just before you fall asleep in the snow and freeze to death."[3]

After logging a successful day on a new eating plan, value that win and build on it.

Value and build on the first couple of workouts at the gym.

In sales, when you've invested the hard work to land a new account, build on that. Salespeople who turn a new customer "win" into a delighted customer "winning streak" of referrals, repeat business, and up-selling, produce superior results.

One of the other ways momentum helps is by inspiring others—and others return the favor. As Kanter says, "Moods are catching... 'Primitive emotional contagion' is the unconscious tendency to mimic another person's facial expressions, tone of voice, posture, and movements, even when one is focused on other things and is seemingly unaware of the model for the mood."[4]

When people experience wins and share them with others, the excitement is contagious and comes right back to the source. Often without realizing it, others become encouragers, supporters, and cheerleaders, just because they are picking up on someone's enthusiasm.

> "Success breeds success. People want to be involved with things that are successful, that are moving forward."
> Jody Williams, activist and Nobel Peace Prize winner

Truly, positive momentum is one of the great allies in overcoming inertia. It needs to be valued.

2. Follow wins with vigorous action

The most important way to turn a win into a winning streak is to follow wins with vigorous

action.

The best time to make another sales call is right after a sale. Often after a big win,

> *"I'm a firm believer in luck. The harder I work the luckier I get."*
> Coach Dick Motta

out comes the champagne. Instead, if salespeople invest extra time using the momentum from the sale to generate enthusiasm in prospects, a disproportionate impact can be gained from the small amount of time invested.

The best time to prepare a presentation is right after giving a successful one. When enthusiasm is high and creativity is flowing, production comes quickly, with high quality.

The best time to tackle another improvement is immediately after successfully implementing one, while still seeing the benefits. The excitement felt from past improvement makes it easier to swallow the new change and maintain forward progress.

APPLY: Celebrate some wins

Years ago I heard someone say, "You can be winning but feel like you're losing if you don't keep score." When we are fighting inertia and seeking to turn wins into winning streaks, it is vital that we sniff out, identify, and celebrate every win.

Take a few minutes to identify your wins. What have you done right? What positive changes have you made? How have you moved forward? Write them down. Begin by celebrating those wins!

What are some wins I should celebrate?

1 _____

2 _____

3 _____

4 _____

5 _____

APPLY: Take vigorous action

Now take your most important win. How can you follow it with vigorous action?

Take a minute to identify one action you will take to hit the thrusters and turn your win into a winning streak.

Top win:

_____

What vigorous action will I follow it with?

_____

When will I do it?

_____

QUICK TIP FOR SALES PROFESSIONALS

Be ready to share your good news.

Identify one piece of fantastic, recent news that you want to have on the tip of your tongue when talking with customers and prospects:

_____

_____

_____

_____

_____

HABITS
Get better one habit at a time

"Life patterns have a funny way of creating a momentum that is difficult to alter. You need to take control of your patterns, and not let your patterns control you."

Charles Platkin, author of Breaking The Pattern

Habits put us on autopilot

Most daily decisions are automatic. A person doesn't have to relearn how to brush their teeth, tie their shoes, or use a fork. They don't relearn how to drive, interact with others, or how to answer a cell phone.

Habits are a good thing

Habits are very helpful, but often get a bad rap. When someone hears the word "habit," the tendency is to think about *bad patterns that need to be changed.* But habits themselves are extremely useful.

A habit, once established, begins to govern daily actions.

Habits enable people to focus conscious energy on other activities. Imagine how little would be accomplished if common routines had to be relearned every day.

> *"I am your constant companion. I am your greatest helper or heaviest burden. I will push you onward and upward, or drag you down to failure. I am completely at your command. 90% of the things you do might just as well be turned over to me and I will be able to do them quickly and correctly. I am easily managed. Show me exactly how you want something done and after a few lessons I will do it automatically. I am the servant of all great people and alas! of all failures as well. I am not a machine, although I work with all the precision of a machine, plus the intelligence of a man. You can run me for profit or run me for ruin—it makes no difference to me. Take me, train me, be firm with me and I will place the world at your feet. Be easy with me and I will destroy you. Who am I? I am Habit."*
>
> Anonymous[1]

Paying the price to get better results

Motivator Les Brown says, "To achieve something that you have never achieved before, you must *become* someone that you have never *been* before."

This happens by improving daily habits.

Debbie Ford articulates well the price to pay in changing habits: "What each of us needs to cultivate in order to ensure our success is self-discipline. Discipline by definition means training that produces moral or mental improvement. Its job is to bring orderliness to our lives…. Discipline… supports us in staying true to what's really important and making sure we achieve our goals. But for some of us, the fear of discipline will be one of the biggest roadblocks we face…. Afraid that we will be constrained, confined, or controlled, many of us resist discipline at all costs. We allow the defiant seven-year-old inside of us to take the reins and operate our lives under the motto Nobody's Going to Tell Me What to Do…. People are constantly whining to me, 'But, Debbie, it's so hard.' But it's not so hard. What's hard is living with yourself when you don't do what you say you are going to do."[2]

> "My doctor suggested a triple bypass… bars, restaurants, and bakeries."
> Dean Martin

One of the ways to make long-term results permanent is by examining and improving old habits. The key to improvement lies in making small, sustainable changes that can, in time, lead to significant growth.

Replace old habits with better ones

This strategy is a particularly powerful one, for once in place, new habits benefit us for years to come. This strategy of getting better, one new habit at a time, is a tangible way to benefit from goal-setting, beyond the achievement of the goal itself. As new habits are established, behavior changes permanently and benefits compound.

> "The first and best victory is to conquer self."
> Plato

Let's explore a process that can help us replace old habits with better ones.

1. EVALUATE: Be brutally honest about your current habits

The process of replacing habits begins by evaluating current ones in a brutally honest and *non-judgmental* way. Charles Platkin, author of *Breaking The Pattern,* writes, "Working on yourself so that you can achieve meaningful goals and have the life you want isn't easy. Negative or undermining patterns can be deeply ingrained and hard to overcome. You need both motivation and discipline for the task. But to rid yourself of negative patterns, you must first be willing to look unflinchingly at yourself."[3]

Do some evaluation.

Think about the patterns that have brought you the results you are currently getting in your goal area. While you certainly have some positive patterns, for now, focus on the negative ones—the patterns that weigh you down and prevent you from getting the results you truly want. Here are some questions to get you going. Remember to ask them in an honest and *non-judgmental* way:

- What negative *behavior, attitude, and relational* patterns are contributing to your sub-par results?
- What "prices" have you been unwilling to "pay" to achieve your desired results?
- What *little things* do you allow yourself that have *added up* to sub-par results?

APPLY: Capture your evaluation

Now take a few moments to capture your most important responses to the above questions. This honest evaluation is the starting place to crafting new and more forwarding habits.

_____

_____

_____

2. IDENTIFY: Specify the new habit to establish

After we have a realistic understanding of the habits that have contributed to past results, we can identify a new habit to replace them. This is where it gets exciting, because _the past does not equal the future_ when we consciously act to change our patterns.

If drinking soda packs too many calories, we can replace it with diet cola. One pattern change like this adds up. If we drink two sodas daily, we are consuming nearly 2,000 calories per week— more than 100,000 calories in a year. This one pattern change would result in weight loss of _28 pounds in a year._

QUICK TIP FOR SALES PROFESSIONALS

Identify and change your worst habit.

What is your worst habit that undermines better sales results? What new habit will you replace it with? When will you start practicing the new habit?

_____

_____

_____

There are literally hundreds of new habits that can be established. What matters is getting *specific*. Ask yourself, "What new habit should I put in place right now?"

Here are some tips in selecting your new habit:

First, choose a habit that is *simple*. The simpler the behavior, the easier to execute it.

Second, choose a habit that is *sustainable*. As Platkin says, make sure the change is something "you can live with for the rest of your life."

Finally, choose a habit that *fits you*. During a coaching session with sales managers, one of the managers said she was going to start writing notes of encouragement to her people. The problem was that she *was not a writer*. Her communication style was verbal and she stayed in touch with her people by phone daily. Rather than establishing a note-writing habit, I suggested she focus on *verbal encouragement during phone conversations* because that would fit her communication style. Because this fits her style more, it is an easier habit to sustain. Likewise, make sure the new habit you are considering fits *you*.

3. ACQUIRE: Practice until the behavior becomes habit

After selecting the new habit, practice the new behavior until it becomes automatic. It takes some time to turn a new *behavior* into a *habit*.

Here's the good news: establishing a new habit takes time, but it doesn't

> *Establishing a new habit takes time, but it doesn't take forever.*

take *forever*. Experts say that new habits take between 21 and 90 days to establish. Then they become automatic. After that, we don't have to consciously think about them.

One of the national experts on this topic is Tony Schwartz. Schwartz co-authored *The Art of the Deal* with Donald Trump, and *The Power of Full Engagement* with Jim Lohr. In *Engagement,* the authors point out that "great performers, whether they are athletes or fighter pilots, surgeons or Special Forces soldiers, FBI agents or CEOs, all rely on positive rituals to manage their energy and achieve their goals."[4] When I spoke with Tony Schwartz about this, I asked him how long, realistically, these new habits take to acquire. He said, "It varies, but the bigger ones take *at most 90 days.*"[5]

> "Mastery may be easier than you think."
> Brian Tracy

APPLY: Change a habit and benefit forever

So what will it be? What new habit do you want to begin putting in place, right now?

Remember, this strategy of getting better, one new habit at a time, is one of the great benefits of pursuing goals. By replacing old habits with better ones, changes are made that will benefit us for years to come.

Take a few minutes to identify the new habit you're going to put into place, how long it will take to establish, and when you will begin.

New habit: _____

_____

How long will it take to establish (21-90 days)? _____

When will I begin? _____

Stick With It

BIG CHANGE
Make a big strategy change when necessary

"The winds and waves are always on the side of the ablest navigators."

Edward Gibbon, British historian

Dogged persistence *and* flexibility
Dogged persistence is usually needed to break out of inertia. But occasionally a big strategy change is in order.

Ironically, breaking out of inertia to win big prizes requires a powerful combination of both dogged persistence and flexibility.

This is a dogged persistence that is open minded and willing to try new strategies. This is flexibility that follows through. *This combination is very, very powerful.*

Surprising words from a successful venture capitalist
Launching a new business requires this unique combination. And venture capitalists look for entrepreneurs who possess it.

One of our investors is a seasoned businessman who has put money into three dozen start-ups. Roughly one-third of his picks have survived—an outstanding record. His best choice has produced a 65-fold return on his investment.

In the early days of our company, we met over coffee and I asked him what he had learned about successful start-ups. Specifically, I asked him what separates the companies that survive from those that don't.

Without hesitation he said, "Leadership." I asked, "What type of leadership?" Again, without hesitation, he said, "They have two qualities—they will not give up *and* they don't have too big of an ego." He elaborated, "The entrepreneurs who make it are doggedly persistent, but at the same time, when an idea isn't working,

> "When one door closes another door opens; but we so often look so long and so regretfully upon the closed door, that we do not see the ones which open for us."
> Alexander Graham Bell

they're willing to toss it and try new things." My investor friend said it was *this combination* of dogged persistence *with flexibility* that makes successful entrepreneurs win.

Jim Collins observed the same thing in the good-to-great companies he studied: "There is nothing wrong with pursuing a vision for greatness. After all, the good-to-great companies also set out to create greatness. But unlike the comparison companies, the good-to-great companies continually refined the *path* to greatness with the brutal facts of reality."[1]

If we have been working long and hard and aren't breaking out of inertia, a big change may be in order. This is one of the strategies that can be employed.

Warning
Please heed this warning: only apply this strategy *after* working long and hard. Ongoing improvement, coupled with vigorous action, usually gets us where we want to go. Declaring the need for a big strategy change can be an excuse for not doing what we know we should do. But when we have been working hard and consistently and are not achieving the results we expect, it may be time for a big change in strategy.

When is it time for a big change?
Here are some questions that may call for a big change in strategy:

- *Have you been working three or four times as long as you thought you would be?* Strategies always take longer than we initially plan—but they don't take *forever.* Have you been going *much, much* longer than you initially planned?
- *Based on what you now know, when you project into the future, do you think you can "get there from here" with your current strategy?* You have much more knowledge on which to base future projections—leverage it as you think about the future.
- *What have you learned that could play a role in a new strategy?* As Edison worked feverishly to invent an economical light bulb, he famously failed more than 10,000 times along the way. During the journey, reporters asked him if he was frustrated at his thousands of failures. "No, I've simply found thousands of ways *not* to make a light bulb." And he meant it. Edison kept a detailed log of each attempt, and leveraged

the failed attempts to narrow his focus toward better possibilities. *Use the knowledge you've gained from what hasn't worked to improve future strategies.*

When an "ah-ha moment" leads to breakthrough

Sometimes an "ah-ha moment" leads to a sudden breakthrough. We may have been working very hard when, suddenly, we "see it"—a new insight opens up a brand new window of opportunity.

This is an important part of the story of my friend, Rob Sample. In the mid-1970s, he and some friends launched a company that sold front-edge niche products to financial institutions. They had worked for months, building a book of business that included many small financial institutions. Rob personally had 73 accounts. The problem? The company was scratching by. Rob told me, "Greg, we were surviving. But had we kept doing what we were doing, we never would have achieved the dream."

Rob decided to take a weekend to step back and take a fresh look at his business.

When he walked into the office Monday morning, he knew what needed to be done. He decided to give up 70 of his clients, for they couldn't use his best products. Rob's ideal clients would be large mutual funds that were looking for something unique like he offered.

Rob had two problems. First, he had to call 70 clients and tell them he couldn't serve them anymore. He did this graciously.

The other problem was that he had no large clients to replace them. To find new prospects, he took an industry phone book, opened to a page, put his finger down and landed on one of the nation's largest mutual funds. He laughs now as he recalls that day.

He dialed the number. Amazingly, Rob navigated his way through "the gatekeepers" to the president, and asked for a five-minute appointment. Treating Rob roughly, the president repeatedly said things like, "Do you know who I am?" and "How could you possibly have something I don't already have?"

Rob persisted.

He said, "I'm going to be in your area, and if I could have just five minutes of your time, I think it would be worth it to you." Finally the president gave in. "Five minutes. Not a minute more."

At that point, Rob booked an airline ticket from Seattle to Boston. When he arrived at the prestigious office, he thought to himself, "What am I doing here?!"

When he stepped into the office of the president, the president again informed him, "You have five minutes. Not a minute more."

They ended up meeting for 90 minutes. During the meeting, the president repeatedly said, "You can do that? You can really do that?"

By the time Rob left that office, his business had taken an entirely different trajectory. He would become a personal friend of the president. Their companies would do great volumes of business together over the next twenty years. And the prestige of that new client would open up other leading companies to Rob as well.

The great thing about bad results

The great thing about bad results is that it leads us to ponder our strategy and come up with better solutions. It's been said, "When we succeed we tend to party, but when we fail we tend to ponder."

Tony Robbins says, "Massive, consistent action with pure persistence and a sense of flexibility in pursuing your goals will ultimately give you want you want, but you must abandon any sense that there is no solution."[2]

> "Mickey Mouse popped out of my mind onto a drawing pad 20 years ago on a train ride from Manhattan to Hollywood at a time when business fortunes of my brother Roy and myself were at lowest ebb and disaster seemed right around the corner."
> Walt Disney

APPLY: Is it time for an "ah-ha moment?"

Consider this question: "What have I learned since starting that could help me improve my strategy?" Remember, stepping back and evaluating what *hasn't* worked may lead you to an "ah-ha moment" that catapults you to a *whole new level*.

What hasn't worked as well as planned?

_____

_____

What might work better?

_____

_____

QUICK TIP FOR SALES PROFESSIONALS

Improve a strategy.

What is something you have been doing that, honestly, isn't working?

_____

_____

Decide now to recycle that experience and improve the strategy. What new and improved strategy will you replace it with?

_____

_____

Stick With It

OVERCOMING DISCOURAGEMENT

Winning the most valuable prizes in life requires ardor and persistence, so it is quite normal to become discouraged along the way. In fact, *what we do with discouragement* often makes the difference as to whether or not we ultimately win.

Debbie Ford hits this nerve in her book *The Best Year of Your Life* when she says, "Most of us are unaware of the extreme resignation that is brewing just beneath the surface of our consciousness. The voice of resignation is a little different for each of us, but its tone usually sounds something like this: 'Why bother? It's never going to happen. I don't have what it takes. It's too much work. I don't have time. I can't deal with it. I don't deserve it.' When we fall short where we had hoped to succeed, when our day-to-day lives fail to resemble our visions of what is possible, when our goals haven't turned into reality, our hope for a great life begins to die, our senses deaden, and gradually we become resigned about our futures." [1]

The final seven strategies will help you constructively deal with discouragement so you don't quit, but instead persist until you win your prize!

Stick With It

MOODS
Manage your moods

15

"Emotional power is the skill of coping with your emotions
so they don't interfere with your performance."

Dr. Shane Murphy, sports psychologist

Conquering discouragement from within

Discouragement often comes from within. Achieving goals would
be much easier if people felt upbeat all the time.

But that's not how it is. If feelings were likened to internal
weather, no one experiences balmy, 75-degree weather all the
time.

Managing moods is an important strategy to overcome
negative feelings encountered on the path to achieving goals.

The role of managing moods in performance

In every walk of life and in pursuit of every goal, managing moods
is essential to peak performance.

Harvard's Rosabeth Moss Kanter says, "Athletes and coaches,

entertainers and professionals, know the value of positive "self-talk"—those silent pep talks in the head that keep spirits up and encourage peak performance. Top performers get good at screening out messages

> *"Basketball is more mental than physical."*
> Michael Jordan

that could interfere with their internal pep talk. They concentrate on the task at hand and shut their ears... to anything else."[1]

Michael Jordan said, "Basketball is more mental than physical." Couldn't the same be said about every endeavor? When people get discouraged, everything is harder.

How to manage your moods

How can we manage moods? How can we control our moods rather than be controlled by them?

1. Avoid extremes

A good place to start is by avoiding emotional extremes. Extreme ups and downs work against top performance.

This is surprising because "up feelings" are enjoyable. But balance is more valuable long-term. Because people can't sustain emotional highs, adrenaline junkies set themselves up for an emotional rollercoaster. This proves detrimental to consistent high performance.

> *"Extremes—emotions that wax too intensely or for too long— undermine our stability."*
> Daniel Golemen, author of Emotional Intelligence

This principle was one of Coach Wooden's secrets to sustained success with his college basketball teams. Hall-of-famer Kareem

Abdul-Jabbar said about Coach Wooden, "He discouraged expressing emotion on the court, stressing that it would eventually leave us vulnerable to opponents."[2]

In the coach's words, "I preferred to maintain a gradually increasing level of both achievement and emotions rather than trying to create artificial e m o t i o n a l highs. For every contrived peak you create, there is a subsequent valley. I do not like valleys. Self-control provides emotional stability and few valleys."[3]

> "I believe that for every artificial peak you create, there is a valley. I don't like valleys. Games are lost in valleys. Therefore, I wasn't much for giving speeches to stir up emotions before a game."
> Coach John Wooden

Instead of pursuing emotional *highs* the goal should be emotional *stability*. And rather than being devastated by emotional *lows*, know that "This too will pass."

Sales is a bipolar profession

The sales profession is loaded with extremes. Those of us who sell live for the great feelings that come with landing accounts, closing big deals, and reaching challenging goals.

But beware of the pendulum.

When big wins come, it's important to use that momentum for maximum advantage. But beware of getting swept away in the emotional current.

When disappointing losses come, it's helpful to remember that this is just part of the ebb and flow.

By avoiding both emotional extremes, it's easier to stay on task, working hard and putting in the sustained effort that pays big over time.

QUICK TIP FOR SALES PROFESSIONALS

Sales is a bipolar profession.

Winning in sales often boils down to working in all kinds of emotional weather. In what kind of emotional weather do you typically not put in your very best effort? What can you do to assure a great effort in this situation?

_____

_____

_____

---

2. Focus on what you can control

The second way to manage emotions is by focusing on what can be controlled. Most worries and fears are based on things that cannot be controlled. Energy and focus that could be invested working toward worthwhile goals is often dissipated on what cannot be changed.

There is no use in worrying about a lack of natural talent

> "As the years passed, I was determined not to let those things I couldn't control detract from those things under my control."
> Coach John Wooden

or obsessing about the physical attributes of others. It is an utter waste to lament the special "break" that didn't come, or the college admission letter that didn't materialize. Why waste time thinking about an opportunity that could have been taken or a choice that shouldn't have been made? These "What ifs" should be ignored completely. Focus should be solely on what is under our control. The exception to the rule: When reflection leads to lessons learned. When you've learned, move on, full speed ahead.

> "The big difference between these champions and most of us is that they have learned how to stay cool and focused when the pressure is on."
> Dr. Shane Murphy

Here is a great truth: we can get where we want to go *from where we are right now*. We have what it takes—with what is under our control.

3. Control your thoughts

A final way to manage emotions is by controlling thoughts. While feelings can't be controlled, thoughts can be. And ultimately, thoughts change feelings.

Marriage expert Gary Smalley says, "Don't ignore your feelings. They reveal what you're thinking."

> "The Master... realizes that excelling in sport is a constant tug-of-war between progress and frustration—and that you can't improve unless you go back to the drawing board and patiently work your way through those down cycles when your game seems to be falling apart."
> Mark McCormack, author of
> What They Didn't Teach You in Harvard Business School

Feelings are *indicators of thoughts*.

Feelings of anxiety, discouragement, fear, elation, or excitement are the result of thoughts that are circulating in the mind.

Coach Wooden's approach to controlling thoughts is revealing, "Losing is only temporary and not all-encompassing. You must simply study it, learn from it, and try hard not to lose the same way again. Then you must have the *self-control* to forget about it."[4]

It's all in how we interpret things

Thoughts are often interpretations of events. Changing thoughts, then, often means changing interpretations.

In *Learned Optimism*, Dr. Martin Seligman identifies the critical role interpretation plays in how people feel about their lives. To change the way a person feels, it is first necessary to change their interpretations.

For example, when our company was 18 months old, we were still fighting for survival. At times the task in front of us was daunting; depressing thoughts would flood my mind. Whenever that happened, it was because I was negatively interpreting challenges. Thoughts like, "Maybe our services *aren't* really needed," led to depression and discouragement.

At those key times, I reminded myself that other entrepreneurs also had difficulty launching their businesses. When Howard Schultz pitched his vision for Starbucks to potential investors, he was turned down by more than 200 people in his quest for capital.

Those stories buoyed me because they helped me interpret my situation differently. I could tell myself, "All great new ventures take time to catch on. This is normal." That interpretation always lifted my spirits and helped me get back to work.

APPLY: Improve your thoughts

How are your thoughts? Take a few minutes to evaluate what you are thinking about achieving your goals.

After doing that, consider improving those interpretations. Remember, there are many ways to interpret what has happened. Choose an interpretation that puts you in an optimistic, empowered frame of mind.

Thought / interpretation:

_____

Better thought / interpretation:

_____

Possible impact on my feelings:

_____

Stick With It

EXPECT
Expect to prevail

16

"I will study and prepare myself and someday
my chance will come."

Abraham Lincoln

Self-fulfilling prophecy

One of the ways to overcome discouragement is by expecting to prevail. Disappointment is normal. But *expecting to prevail becomes a self-fulfilling prophecy.* When people expect to prevail, they prevail more often. Winning increases confidence and gives assurance of future wins and the cycle continues.

> *"Perpetual optimism is a force multiplier."*
> Colin Powell

Since expecting to prevail is a self-fulfilling prophecy, let's put it to work for us. Let's expect to prevail!

How does positive expectancy lead to prevailing?

Understanding how positive expectancy helps us prevail removes the mystery surrounding it. It also helps us see that we have every reason to expect that *we will* prevail.

1. Expectancy stirs us to PREPARE

Positive expectancy helps people prevail by stirring them to prepare to win.

When expectancy is missing so is the desire to work hard. Failure is certain if winning isn't a reasonable expectation. On the other hand, when someone expects to prevail, they put in the extra effort that assures their best possible performance. That effort may be the very thing that pushes them over the top.

The blockbuster film, *My Big Fat Greek Wedding,* wouldn't have materialized had Nia Vardalos not maintained positive expectancy about her dream for the movie against very long odds. An outsider to Hollywood, she moved to Los Angeles to pursue her goal of making movies.

Many people spoke deadening words to her about her prospects. To one, she responded, *"You* get out my way!" To keep the dream alive, Nia remained active in the comedy circuit, entertaining crowds with the hilarious story of her family.

Because she believed that "if she prepared, someday her chance would come," she wrote

> *"Luck affects everything. Let your hook always be cast; in the stream where you least expect it there will be a fish."*
> Ovid

the movie script and kept it with her. One evening after her act, actress Rita Wilson approached her. Wilson had grown up in a similarly animated family and absolutely loved the show. She told Vardalos that it should be a movie and that she wanted to see a script. Vardalos responded, "I have one right here."

Rita Wilson gave the script to her husband, Tom Hanks, whose production company took on the project. *My Big Fat Greek Wedding* went on to become one of the most successful word-of-mouth movies in the history of cinema.

Selling boats in a snowstorm

When someone expects to prevail, they keep showing up. They keep putting in their best effort. Over time, this persistence pays off.

For those of us who sell, it is easy to make excuses about…

- Selling on Monday mornings
- Selling on Friday afternoons
- Selling in the middle of the week
- Selling during the holidays
- Etc., etc., etc…

These excuses drive sales manager crazy.

But when we expect fish to bite, like avid fisherman, we can't wait to get our line in the water regardless of what day it is.

Three winters ago, the Seattle area shut down because of a snowstorm. Virtually every business closed and the roads were empty. I went to my office and made calls to clients and prospects in other parts of the country.

In the afternoon I made a call to the local boat dealer where we purchased our boat. Not until after they answered the phone, did it dawn on me that they were probably short-staffed because of the snow.

I mentioned to Kirk Benson, the sales manager, that he

probably had no salespeople that day. His response, "No, actually, all of my salespeople are here." I hung up the phone very impressed. I started thinking about it. Few—if any—people would show up on the boat lot that day. But anyone who *did* would certainly be serious about buying a boat! That perspective must have motivated his people to get to work when most people stayed home.

Whether or not any boats were sold that day, that kind of positive expectancy leads to superior preparation and performance day after day. Over time it pays off.

QUICK TIP FOR SALES PROFESSIONALS

Expect to prevail all the time.

What days—or what *time* of day—do you lower your expectation for success?

_____

_____

Destroy those limitations and raise your level of play by choosing to expect the best every hour you are working.

---

2. Expectancy attracts THE HELP OF OTHERS

Another way positive expectancy works is by attracting the help of others. People begin offering assistance, support, and encouragement; they join our cause.

Positive expectancy creates a gravitational pull that draws others into our venture. As Colin Powell says, "Perpetual optimism is a force multiplier."

One key task of leadership is developing confidence in others *before winning*. Leaders must inspire others to believe—and their belief helps make it reality.

Leaders maintain positive expectancy even when external circumstances don't warrant it. A *Fortune Magazine* Q&A article with Bill Gates in early 2003 says it all: "In the gloom of the tech world, America's richest man sees good things ahead."[1]

Craig Venter heads Celera Genomics, one of the leading organizations decoding the human genome. Craig shows his expectancy in how he takes risks, "Craig likes to take high dives into empty pools. He tries to time it so the water is there by the time he hits the bottom."[2] This kind of expectancy attracts the help of others—which is essential to reaching his ambitious goal.

In the same way, our own perpetual optimism is a force multiplier. As we expect to prevail, we attract friends, family, colleagues, prospects, and customers to help us.

3. Expectancy keeps OUR HEAD IN THE GAME

A final way expectancy helps people prevail is by keeping their head in the game. Winning requires constant effort. When people expect to prevail, they keep pushing, improving, and going the extra mile.

In the 2006 Rose Bowl, top-ranked USC faced #2 Texas in what some considered the most dramatic of the 92 Rose Bowls. The favored USC enjoyed most of the pre-game spotlight. Boasting a 34-game winning streak and two consecutive national championships, the Trojans were hailed by many as the greatest college team in decades.

During the game, they did not disappoint. With less than

seven minutes to play USC led by twelve points. It appeared the Trojans would live up to all of the media hype.

But the Texas Longhorns kept their heads in the game. Uber-athlete Vince Young rallied Texas to score 15 points in the final four minutes. Young's final eight-yard touchdown scramble, with 19 seconds left, capped a dramatic upset that brought Texas their first national championship in 35 years.

Behind this remarkable comeback was an unbeatable positive expectancy. Throughout the game, even in the darkest moments, the Longhorns believed they would win. Coach

> "It was surreal sitting there in the fourth quarter down 12 points and you still think you're going to win. We never really thought we were going to lose the game. We never got discouraged."
> Mack Brown, Texas Longhorns' coach

Mack Brown said later, "It was surreal sitting there in the fourth quarter down 12 points and you still think you're going to win. We never really thought we were going to lose the game. We never got discouraged."[3]

If we think back over past losses, how many of them could have been turned into wins had we just kept our head in the game?

APPLY: Write a self-fulfilling prophecy

Since positive expectancy is a self-fulfilling prophecy, we might as well write the prophecy ourselves.

You have every reason to expect to prevail. So expect to prevail! Craft a fresh, self-fulfilling prophecy about why you *can* and *will* prevail.

Why I will prevail:

_____

_____

_____

_____

_____

Stick With It

BE REALISTIC
Be realistic about how long it takes

"He who would leap high must take a long run."

Danish proverb

When it seems like forever!

One of the greatest discouragements is the sense that it's taking forever to reach our goals. It is said that, "Hope deferred makes the heart sick."

While *bold* goals motivate people, *overreaching* can cause a complete shutdown. When goals feel impossible to reach, disillusionment creeps in, followed by a "What's the use?" attitude.

When this happens, the strategy to employ is *realism*. Goals must be injected with a fresh dose of realism about how long the process will take. This restatement of goals reengages the drive to achieve it.

Balance boldness with realism

It's important to delicately balance *boldness* and *realism*. Daniel Goleman describes this balance in *Emotional Intelligence*: "People seem to concentrate best when the demands on them are a bit greater than usual.... If there is too little demand on them, people are bored. If there is too much to handle, they get anxious. Flow occurs in the delicate zone between boredom and anxiety."[1]

Guy Kowasaki says what's needed is a "telescope" and a "microscope." The telescope is the ability to see an exciting vision. The microscope is the ability to analyze things closely and realistically. Says Kowasaki, "When telescopes work, everyone is an astronomer, and the world is full of stars. When they don't, everyone whips out the microscopes, and the world is full of flaws. The reality is that you need both microscopes and telescopes to achieve success."[2]

Two questions to inject realism into our goals

When it's taking much longer than anticipated for plans to take shape and discouragement is sinking in, it may be time to inject a fresh dose of realism into our goals. Our responses to two questions will help us restate our goals more realistically.

> *Sound assumptions are the key to setting realistic goals.*
> Larry Bossidy and Ram Charan, in Execution

1. Is it under my control?

It's unrealistic to pursue a goal that isn't under our control.

We can't control our weight. But we *can* control our calorie intake.

We can't control how many new accounts we close. But we *can* control how many calls we make.

We can't control whether we win the gold medal, but we *can* control our training regimen.

Sports psychologist Shane Murphy observed a key difference between gold medal winners and their contenders. Contenders tend to stay focused on *results* goals, while winners translate those into *action* goals. Murphy points out that the best athletes are able to focus when the pressure is on, partly because they focus on what is under their control. Their competitors feel more stress because they are distracted by factors outside their control, such as what their competitors are doing.

This was poignantly illustrated in the 2002 winter Olympics when dark-horse Sarah Hughes gave a flawless performance in women's figure-skating. Sarah's relaxed and joyful performance garnered her the gold medal. Afterward she said, "I just went out and had fun." Her perspective contrasted starkly with a favored contender, who was visibly stressed prior to the match, as she obsessed about the gold medal that most expected her to win.

A "result" goal is what we ultimately hope to achieve, whether a gold medal, a sales number, a successful business launch, or a desired weight. But like gold medal winners, it is best for us to also establish—*and to focus on*—the "action" goals that are under our control. *Action* goals—like a training regimen, number of prospects to call, or a daily calorie intake limit, put us in control. And they increase the likelihood we will achieve our *results* goals.

QUICK TIP FOR SALES PROFESSIONALS

Make sure you have clear action goals.

Results goals are the end results we want to achieve. They are usually outside our control. *Action* goals, in contrast, are under our control and show us what to do today. How clear are your action goals? If not clear enough, how can you restate them to make them clearer?

_____

_____

_____

_____

---

2. Have I given myself enough time?

We usually under-estimate how long it will take to accomplish our goal. Keith Ellis writes in *The Magic Lamp*, "As a rule of thumb, success will take longer than you think. Everything worthwhile in life seems to take longer than we want it to."[3]

Most goals are reachable *if given more time*. Most financial, personal, relational, and health goals, as well as most worthwhile corporate initiatives are reachable if people stay with them longer.

> *"A lot of entrepreneurs run screaming as soon as things get tough… Many companies have turned away too quickly and walked away from an opportunity when success was just around the corner."*
> William Crookston,
> Professor of entrepreneurship, USC

Sometimes the problem isn't the size of the goal, but *its*

timeframe.

This problem is so common in corporations that it has birthed the cliché "flavor of the month." Many corporate initiatives become "flavor of the month" simply because they are not focused on long enough to take hold in the company.

In contrast, when leaders persist and give their vision time to grow and succeed over time, results compound.

One business leader who is accomplishing such a feat is Jerry Baker, CEO of First Horizon Financial. First Horizon is an innovative leader in the mortgage industry. Mr. Baker is a big reason First Horizon has such bright prospects for the future. A decade ago he developed and began gradually implementing a new strategy called "All Things Financial." This new platform revolutionizes the value First Horizon loan officers provide their customers.

With patience and persistence, Jerry Baker has continued building the structure, culture, and incentive system to make the new value proposition attractive to employee and customer alike. Mr. Baker remained steady despite fads passing through the industry on the one side and the inertia of tradition on the other.

But like a snowball tumbling downhill, picking up speed and size with every turn, Baker's vision for First Horizon is becoming reality in ever-more-exciting ways, and First Horizon is positioned to provide leadership in this rapidly changing industry.

> *"I didn't overreach. We just kept moving it forward, and gave it time to catch on."*
> Jerry Baker, CEO First Horizon Financial

I recently asked Jerry Baker how he sustained his vision over the years and prevented it from becoming "flavor of the month." His response was telling, "I didn't overreach. We just kept moving it forward, and gave it time to catch on."[4]

The same is true with our personal goals. We would benefit greatly by applying Jerry Baker's wisdom to whatever goal we are pursuing, telling ourselves, "I won't overreach. I will just keep moving it forward, and give it time to work."

You are closer than when you began

When you feel like throwing in the towel because you're nowhere near where you wanted to be at this point, be encouraged. You are much *closer* to your goal than you were when you started.

When we launch into a new goal we envision a much quicker path to completion. But when we get into the work, we begin to realize the path is much longer. For example, we

> "The road to success is always under construction."
> Lily Tomlin, actress

may discover that what we thought would take a month will take a quarter. What we hoped would take two years ends up requiring five. This is disheartening because *it makes us feel further from our goal than when we began.*

But what disheartens people is not the hard work they put in. What discourages is the sense of getting further from a goal despite best efforts. The reality is not that the goal is farther away. Instead, the goal-setter has a much better understanding of how long it will take and is actually closer to real, not imagined, achievement.

It is like swimming across a river.

Imagine standing on one side of a wide river and saying to yourself, "I can swim across this river. No problem." Then you dive in.

If you've done any swimming at all, you know that swimming is much more arduous than it appears. After ten minutes, you are exhausted, and as you look to a still distant shore, you realize that you have a long, long way to go. Suddenly your confidence ebbs. And now it feels like you have a longer distance in front of you than when you stood

> *"The middle of every successful project looks like a disaster."*
> Rosabeth Moss Kanter

comfortably on the riverbank, envisioning crossing to the other side. In fact, you may begin to wonder at this point if you'll make it across at all.

But you aren't farther behind.

In fact, you have come a long way.

If you look back to the shore where you jumped in, you will realize that you have already swam a great distance.

Don't be discouraged by the time it is taking. Harvard's Kanter says, "The middle of every successful project looks like a disaster." Rather than being discouraged, inject a fresh realism about how long it will take, and then strengthen your resolve by remembering how far you have already come.

APPLY: Make your goal more realistic

As you answer the two questions above, do you uncover some "unreality" in your goals? Remember, striking the balance between boldness and realism is the key to unlocking our internal drive. If you need to make your goal more realistic, inject a fresh doze of realism into it today and get working on your new, more realistic goal immediately.

How have I stated my goal?

_____

_____

What is unrealistic about it?

_____

_____

How will I restate it in more realistic terms?

_____

_____

USE FAILURE
Use failure to move forward

"My life has shown that I'm not afraid to fail, that success is achieved by those who don't give up. I'm a guy who has fallen down my whole life. But I've gotten up and wiped the blood off my knees every time."

Antonio Villaraigosa, Mayor of Los Angeles

Failure hurts—and it should

As people strive toward their goals, they fail many times. This hurts. Pain is one of the most common forms of discouragement encountered along the way.

Failure hurts—and it should.

The sting of failure spurs us to find better ways. If failure didn't hurt, we wouldn't work to get better.

It's like the human body's ability to feel and react to physical pain. When a child touches a hot burner, the searing pain makes them pull their hand back immediately. The throbbing pain that lingers reminds them to heed their parent's warning.

In the sales profession, the Gallup Organization discovered something surprising about how top performing salespeople process the pain of failure. The conventional wisdom is that failure doesn't bother top performers as much as average performers. Gallup found the opposite. Top performers actually care *more*. But *they are more likely to springboard from their failure into better approaches.*

Sales trainer Thomas Freese captures this perspective when he says, "I've found that the best way to reduce the pain of failure is by failing less often." Top salespeople feel the pain of failure and use it to spur improvement.

> "The person interested in success has to learn to view failure as a healthy, inevitable part of the process of getting to the top."
> Joyce Brothers

Each of us can employ the same strategy in pursuit of our goals: *use failure to move forward.*

QUICK TIP FOR SALES PROFESSIONALS

Feel the pain and use it to get better.

What is a failure that still stings?

_____

How have you used that failure to get better?

_____

How can you squeeze even more benefit from it to further improve your strategies?

_____

Rewarding a $50 million failure

In *Jack—Straight From The Gut,* former CEO Jack Welch told a story about how General Electric rewarded a $50 million failure. In the late 1970s, GE invested big to create an innovative new light bulb called the Halarc Lamp. The new product was environmentally friendly, lasted ten times longer than conventional products and used a fraction of the energy of a traditional bulb. The problem? Customers weren't willing to pay $10.95 for a light bulb, no matter how revolutionary it was.

> *"You have to turn a negative into a positive. You have to defeat defeat. To do this you have to believe in what you do, even when you lose."*
> Andy Reid, Philadelphia Eagles football coach

It was a $50 million swing—and it didn't work.

Instead of punishing the project players, GE actually rewarded the innovators with cash and promotions. Said Welch, "While no one was happy with the results, we made a big point of rewarding the people on the team. We wanted everyone in the company to know that taking a big swing and missing was okay."[1]

Everyone fails along the way to success

Failure floods the mind with debilitating thoughts like, "If this was going to happen, it would come more easily." Or, "I bet so-and-so didn't fail this many times when they were doing it."

The fact is, everyone fails on the way to success.

Dr. Seuss's first book, *And to Think That I Saw It on Mulberry Street,* was turned down by 23 publishers before going to print.

J.D. Salinger received even more rejections when he sought a publisher for *Catcher in the Rye.* He kept his more than 30 rejection notices in a drawer as a reminder to press on.

> *"Success is the ability to go from failure to failure without losing your enthusiasm."*
> Winston Churchill

Boxer *Gene Tunney* broke both hands before becoming a professional boxer. Realizing that he could not become a champion through power punching, he retrained himself to become one of the most *highly skilled* boxers ever. He eventually won the world heavyweight championship by beating Jack Dempsey.

Actor Bruce Willis stuttered as a young man.

Sam Walton, founder of Wal-Mart, became energized by failures through a simple discipline. When he made a mistake, he wouldn't waste time beating himself up over it. Instead, he made a relevant improvement the very next morning.

Most grand masters in chess invest at least 15 years learning moves, combinations, and honing skills before winning their first world title.

Director Oliver Stone spent 14 years planning the movie *Alexander.* Despite his past successes and the hype surrounding the movie, it was a big disappointment. Even a director with his success and stature has projects where he has to scratch his head afterward and say, "Well, let's move on to the next one. I guess that one didn't go as well as I hoped."

Geoffrey Canada is the CEO of Harlem Children's Zone. At twelve, he sliced his finger with a knife that he carried for protection in his rough neighborhood. The cut didn't heal properly and he kept it a secret. Now it inspires him. The crooked finger keeps the urgency of his work with children at the front of his mind.

New York Yankee star Alex Rodriguez gets put out a lot. His ten-year, $252 million contract means that he will be paid $115,971 every time he gets put out. But the Yankees don't pay him for that. They pay him for the hits, the homeruns, and the RBIs. It isn't what he *doesn't* do that earns him his salary. It is what he *does*.

> *"The mystery of life is not solved with success, which is an end in itself, but in failure, in perpetual struggle, in becoming."*
> Patrick White, Australian Nobel Prize winning writer

Likewise, achieving goals is *not about* how many failures we *avoid*. Achieving goals is about pressing through failures to win the prize being contended for.

APPLY: Use your failure to improve your efforts

Learning from our failures is what transforms them into forward-moving experiences. Alduous Huxley said, "Experience is not what happens to a man, it is what a man does with what happens to him."

Napoleon Hill, in more than 20 years interviewing successful people about what helped them win, found they all viewed setbacks in the same way. Every one believed that every failure contains a seed that will result in greater advantage. They all viewed failure as a way to benefit.

> *"Failure is a stepping stone, not a tombstone."*
> Theodore Bryant

Coach Vince Lombardi said, "Prosperity is a great teacher; adversity is greater." What is adversity teaching *you*?

In *Peak Performance*, Charles Garfield points out that in the Apollo moon missions, the rockets were off course 90% of the time. The scientists repeatedly made adjustments to keep the rockets on course.

Personal failures play out the same way. Failure is simply feedback on our efforts. Like the Apollo rockets, we may be off course 90% of the time on the way to achieving our goals. But the feedback and course corrections get us there.

Take a few minutes to make some course corrections. Use a recent failure as a way to make corrections that you can put into practice immediately.

Failure: _____

What do I learn from it?

_____

_____

SELF-TALK
Improve your self-talk

"You are today where your thoughts have brought you, you will be tomorrow where your thoughts take you."

Ralph Waldo Emerson

What are you telling yourself?
Without noticing, people talk to themselves all the time.

Drs. Les and Leslie Parrot describe this internal dialogue: "Every one of us, every minute of every hour is holding an unending dialogue with ourselves. A dialogue that colors every experience…. The thoughts are rarely noticed, but they continually shape our attitudes, emotions, and outlook. Our self-talk need not be accurate, in fact for many of us it rarely is. But it never hinders the mind from acting as if it were."

Self-talk is the unending dialogue we have with ourselves.

We engage in self-talk about everything in our lives. We engage in self-talk about our talents, our past, and our opportunities. We engage in self-talk about our successes, our failures, and our struggles.

In fact, our strands of self-talk are like tunes on an iPod, Apple Computer's portable digital media player.

Our brains are like iPods, each with many tunes downloaded. The self-talk in our minds are like the songs we play on our machines. As life's daily activities shape up, our minds select the appropriate self-talk tune and begin playing it in our head.

> *"Inside myself is a place where I live all alone and that's where you renew your springs that never dry up."*
> Pearl S. Buck, American Nobel Prize winning author

Our self-talk shapes what we do next

Stuff happens.

Self-talk shapes what we do next. For example, think about how people handle and respond to a mistake.

When someone makes a mistake, self-talk varies greatly. Consider three different responses to a mistake:

- Person #1: "I *knew* it wasn't going to work out. I should have listened to so-and-so when they said this wasn't a good idea."
- Person #2: "Mistakes are normal. They are part of the process. I'll do better next time."
- Person #3: "I love mistakes because I find my best new ideas through them!"

As you consider these different responses to a mistake, imagine how each one triggers different feelings and actions.

The first person tells himself, "I *knew* it wasn't going to work out. I should have listened to so-and-so when they said this wasn't a good idea." This thought will decrease the motivation to persist. It may even shut them down from further action.

The second person, in contrast, says, "Mistakes are normal. They are part of the process. I'll do better next time." This interpretation keeps them pressing forward.

The third person does even better, telling herself, "I love mistakes, because I find my best new ideas through them!" Her self-talk keeps her pressing on, causing her to squeeze the greatest potential benefit from the mistake.

> *"The most important element in the character of a man who is successful is that of mental toughness."*
> Vince Lombardi

Self-talk shapes what we do next. We can greatly improve our persistence by improving our self-talk. By improving self-talk, we strengthen the mental muscle that supports continuous vigorous action toward a goal.

What is healthy self-talk?

Healthy self-talk empowers a person to take action. *People who are encouraged and taking vigorous action will achieve better results.* Therefore any type of self-talk that shuts us down—whether it is self-talk about us, our past, our job, our location, or the people in our lives—is unhealthy.

Resilience increases as unhealthy areas of self-talk are identified and replaced.

How to improve our self-talk

1. Figure out what you are currently telling yourself

Get real. What are you telling yourself?

Don't gloss over it.

This is the starting place. If you are going to improve your self-talk, you need to know exactly what you are telling yourself... right now.

In *Unleash the Warrior Within*, Richard Machowicz encourages us to take a day and capture our strands of self-talk in a journal. I actually did it for several days. Afterward I took a highlighter to them. I highlighted the positive strands of self-talk in orange, the negative in yellow. Despite how positive and confident I consider myself, I was surprised at how many negative things I was telling myself.

When you write down what you're saying to yourself, you wake up. You look at the statements and realize, "Yea, I *do* tell myself that."

This takes some of the mystery out of negative self-talk.

> *"Self-talk is an often ignored form of communication. Yet, self-talk is probably more responsible for our success or lack of it than any other form of communication."*
>
> Brian Tracy

You realize, "Why do I say that to myself? Where did that come from? I certainly don't have to believe that."

Eleanor Roosevelt said, "No one can make you feel inferior without your consent." Every strand of negative self-talk is a "groove" that we have allowed to be cut in our minds. We can cut new grooves.

APPLY: Capture your self-talk for a day

To record your inner dialogue, keep this book with you. Beginning in the morning, capture every type of "self-talk" relating to achieving your most important goal. Capture everything—*without judgment or evaluation.* At the end of the day, go back and put a plus or minus sign to distinguish between empowering and disempowering thoughts. Don't gloss over the disempowering thoughts. The starting place for improvement is auditing what we already do.

Self-talk for a day
___   _____
___   _____
___   _____
___   _____
___   _____
___   _____
___   _____
___   _____
___   _____
___   _____
___   _____
___   _____
___   _____

2. Decide what you *will* tell yourself

Remember—everything you are currently telling yourself was chosen. Whether consciously or not, *you have chosen* it all.

So you can choose better forms of self-talk now.

Once you've identified a self-limiting statement, you're free to replace it. Returning to the iPod analogy,

> *"Score one for believers in the adage 'use it or lose it.' Targeted mental and physical exercises seem to improve the brain in unexpected ways... Change the input—be it a behavior, a mental exercise... or physical skill—and the brain changes accordingly."*
> Scientific American[1]

once you've identified a tune you don't want anymore, delete it and download a better one.

Make it credible

As we decide what to tell ourselves, we need to craft self-talk that is credible to our minds.

Jim Carrey is one of the best paid actors in Hollywood. But it took him years of persistence to get where he is. This required self-talk that encouraged persistence. He used the example of Rodney Dangerfield as credible evidence that he would eventually make it.

"[Dangerfield] struggled for decades before he reached the top of his profession. I don't know if anybody remembers the era of the comedy club—they were quite popular places at one time, you can only see them now in the Smithsonian, I think—but I did stand-up clubs for fifteen years and sometimes the only thing that kept me going was the thought that Rodney had dropped out of the business when he was thirty but had come back and made it big when he was in his forties. Made it big. In a business that almost always values youth over talent, he was—and still is—absolute proof that it's never too late to make your mark. You may have to quit for a while and sell some aluminum siding, but you don't have to give up your dreams." [2]

Jim Carrey told himself, "Age doesn't matter. I can make it big eventually, if I keep with it." He *could* have told himself, "This industry values youth—I've probably missed my opportunity." But he didn't. Instead, he chose to use Rodney Dangerfield's example as credible evidence, and he built self-talk that encouraged him to persist.

In the same way, find credible evidence to use in creating a realistic piece of self-talk that *your* mind can embrace.

APPLY

Invest a few minutes and identify two pieces of credible evidence on which to build empowering self-talk relative to reaching your goal.

1. _____

2. _____

Make it positive

For self-talk to *empower us to action*, it needs to be stated in the positive, rather than the negative. It needs to *be affirming*.

> "I always wanted to be somebody. I should have been more specific."
> Lily Tomlin, actress

For example, when

crafting a piece of self-talk about how to handle mistakes, say something like, "I love mistakes, because I often find my best new ideas through them." This is much better than phrases like, "I don't let mistakes bother me." While both of these phrases get at the same goal, the positively stated term *empowers us to take action.*

APPLY
Take a minute to refine your self-talk statements so they empower you to take positive action.

1. _____

   _____

2. _____

   _____

Make it present-tense
For self-talk to shape our behavior today, it needs to be stated in the present tense.

To handle mistakes better, a new piece of self-talk should be crafted to tell the mind how it's done now. Replace intentions with action words. For example, instead of saying, "I *will* benefit from mistakes...," say, "*I benefit* from *mistakes....*"

APPLY

Take a minute to refine the wording, making it present tense. Be sure it states *now* what you want to affirm. This present-tense statement instructs your mind to act in the new way immediately!

My new self-talk

1. _____

_____

2. _____

_____

QUICK TIP FOR SALES PROFESSIONALS

Design a phrase to get "in the zone" before each sales call.

Identify a simple, empowering phrase like "Let's go!" or "They need what I have to offer!" to enthusiastically say to yourself right before each call to get you ready to perform at your best.

_____

_____

Practice, practice, practice

To make a new groove in the mind, consciously practice new self-talk until it becomes automatic.

Those practicing new self-talk have to get over the "corniness factor." You may remember Al Franken's corny character, Stuart Smalley, on *Saturday Night Live* and his mantra, "I'm good enough, I'm smart enough, and gosh darn it, people like me!"

We need to realize this fact: we are constantly talking to ourselves anyway. We can *decide* to talk to ourselves in ways that empower us to live our best life.

> "*If you would perfect your body; guard your mind. If you would renew your body, beautify your mind. Strong, pure, and happy thoughts build up the body in vigor and grace.*"
> James Allen, author of As a Man Thinketh

There are so many places to practice self-talk scripts: during commutes, workouts, walks, or right before a meeting or presentation. Practicing better self-talk improves performance immediately in the areas where work is being focused.

Self-talk is a habit of the mind. Like other habits, new self-talk takes time to acquire, but it doesn't take forever.

Ten Empowering Truths

You have every right to believe each of these. Make them your own.

1) I feel the fear and act anyway. This is a sign of my courage.

2) I build upon past wins and turn them into winning streaks.

3) I recycle past losses into something highly usable.

4) I relish my disadvantages because they make my ultimate victory sweeter.

5) I am grateful to be alive. Today is full of beauty, sweetness, joy, and opportunity.

6) I recover quickly. When I fall down, I bounce back and keep going.

7) I have stamina and persistence that will get where I want to be.

8) I get better constantly—and I ultimately win because of it.

9) I relish the growth that comes from challenging goals.

10) I win and use my wins to stretch me to pursue bigger prizes in the future.

ENERGY
Give yourself the energy to follow through

"Fatigue doth make cowards of us all."

Brian Tracy

Keeping fuel in the engine

Sometimes, we "lose steam" in working toward our goals simply because our engine lacks the fuel.

The world, our potential, and our future all look very different

> *"A high energy level can make up for a multitude of shortcomings."*
>
> Len Serafino, author of Sales Talk

when we are fully energized. Give yourself the energy to follow through.

Energy: The most precious resource

I have enjoyed conversing with energy expert, Tony Schwartz, in his home in northern New York City. It has been instructive for me to observe his creation of an environment and schedule that enable him to maximize his energy for peak performance.

In *The Power of Full Engagement,* Tony Schwartz and Jim Lohr share profound insights about how depleted our personal energy levels are today:

"We live in digital time. Our rhythms are rushed, rapid fire and relentless, our days carved up into bits and bytes. We celebrate breadth rather than depth, quick reaction more than considered reflection. We skim across the surface, alighting for brief moments at dozens of destinations but rarely remaining for long at any one. We race through our lives without pausing to consider who we really want to be or where we really want to go. We're wired up but we're melting down.

"Most of us are just trying to do the best that we can. When demand exceeds our capacity, we begin to make expedient choices that get us through our days and nights, but take a toll over time. We survive on too little sleep, wolf down fast foods on the run, fuel up with coffee and cool down with alcohol and sleeping pills. Faced with relentless demands at work, we become short-tempered and easily distracted. We return home from long days at work feeling exhausted and often experience our families not as a source of joy and renewal, but as one more demand in an already overburdened life....

"We use words like obsessed, crazed, and overwhelmed not to describe insanity, but instead to characterize our everyday lives. Feeling starved for time, we assume that we have no choice but to cram as much as possible into every day. But managing time efficiently is no guarantee that we will bring sufficient energy to whatever it is we are doing."[1]

Energy is our most precious resource.

When energized, we take setbacks in stride.

When energized, we remain focused, creative, and resilient.

154

David Petraeus is a Lt. General in the US Army. He commanded the 101st Airborne Division as Baghdad, Iraq fell. Says the General, "Physical and mental toughness are... essential [to] leadership. It's hard to lead from the front if you are in the rear of the formation."

> *"To be fully engaged, we must be physically energized... Full engagement begins with feeling eager to get to work in the morning, equally happy to return home in the evening and capable of setting clear boundaries between the two."*
> Jim Lohr and Tony Schwartz

It's hard to follow through on any goal if we are physically weary. Sometimes what we need is more energy.

Energy exploration:
Places to find renewable energy

Let's do some energy exploration. Sources of energy are right under our feet. Don't treat these as *have-to's*. Instead, view each of these as unique sources of energy that we can benefit from within days if we aren't currently tapping them.

1. Sleep

Sleep is the most basic—and often neglected—source of personal energy. In the year 2000, Americans, on average, were sleeping seven hours per night. A century earlier, we were sleeping eight. Yet our bodies haven't changed. This adds up to a growing sleep deficit.

Study after study confirms that young and old require certain amounts of sleep—and this is unalterable. Despite best efforts to "cheat sleep," it can't be done. Lack of sleep manifests in irritability, negative health effects, and lower productivity.

60% of Americans endure sleep disorders of some kind.

Dr. Bob Arnot is so convinced that good sleep is foundational to personal wellness that while generally discouraging medication, he encourages it if that is the only way to assure proper sleep.[2]

Winston Churchill was an ardent believer in the role proper sleep plays in performance. Churchill said, "You must sleep some time between lunch and dinner and no halfway measures. Take off your clothes and get into bed. That's what I always do. Don't think you will be doing less work because you sleep during the day. That's a foolish notion…You will accomplish more."

If you haven't been getting the rest you need, you may be amazed at how refreshed you feel after two or three nights of great sleep.

Sleep Tips

Here are some quick tips to maximize your sleep:

- Don't short-change yourself. If you need nine hours, give yourself nine. It will repay you in productivity.
- Go to bed and get up at the same time. Our bodies release hormones that help us awaken in the morning and fall asleep at night. This system operates on a 24-hour cycle and works optimally when we are consistent. This is why we experience "jet lag" when traveling across time zones.
- Give your body rest from digestion when you sleep. Eating heavy meals before bed overtaxes your body at night. Eat earlier and let your body rest and renew itself.

2. Exercise

Exercise is an obvious way to increase our energy. But we may want to utilize it more strategically.

Jerry Seinfeld did.

Seinfeld's big break came when he was invited to appear on Johnny Carson's show. To prepare for the several minute monologue, Seinfeld did two things almost obsessively.

First, he practiced his monologue more than 100 times.

Secondly, he put in many extra miles running leading up to his appearance. He used exercise to raise his energy level for that key performance.

We can do the same thing. We can utilize exercise prior to a big meeting, presentation, or event where a heightened energy level will serve us well.

3. Laughter

When we need more energy, laughter can be a great source. The authors of *Improvise This!* say, "Finding humor in your life and being humorous have tremendous value. Laughter is to our mental health what physical exercise is to our body. Same benefits, minus the Stairmaster."[3]

Isn't it amazing how energizing it is to be around funny people?

Wholesome humor—the kind that isn't cynical or degrading—can be an enjoyable source of renewable energy.

4. Down-time

Down-time is another big source of energy renewal. Schwartz and Lohr maintain, "We live in a world that celebrates work and activity, ignores renewal and recovery, and fails to recognize that both are necessary for sustained high performance."[4]

Physiologist Martin Moore-Ede, president of Circadian Technologies says, "At the heart of the problem is a fundamental conflict between the demands of our man-made civilization and the very design of the human brain and body.... We are *machine-centered* in our thinking—focused on the optimization of technology and equipment—rather than *human-centered*—focused on the optimization of human alertness and performance."

Some historians believe the development of the trans-continental railroad marked the shift in American society from an agrarian culture to a machine-based one. The agrarian culture worked in harmony with the seasons. The second, the machine-based culture, began operating around the clock, divorced from the natural rhythms of nature.[5]

Mark McCormack, author of *What They Don't Teach You in Harvard Business School*, took a cue from the top athletes he worked with for years. He would push himself hard for approximately ten weeks, following the hard push with down-time. This rhythm enabled him to raise his level of play and then recuperate.[6]

Planning our down-time—a regular day off or an upcoming vacation—allows us the emotional benefit of *looking forward* to it. Some of us aren't extracting the greatest possible benefit from down-times because we don't plan them in advance.

Let me ask you: what down-times have you built into your schedule? *What are you looking forward to?*

Down-time isn't a luxury—it is critical for high energy. Increase your energy by giving yourself great down-time to look forward to.

APPLY: Give yourself the gift of down-time

Are you looking forward to something in the *next seven days*? If not, identify something right now that you can look forward to. Don't wait to plan it later, because part of the energy that comes from down-time is *anticipating it.*

Do you have a fun getaway or vacation scheduled for the *next six months*? If not, plan something now. Jot down a list of a few ideas and block out the time and do it. If you are married, call your spouse and surprise them! Give yourself something to look forward to—and enjoy the energy that comes from looking forward to it!

I am looking forward to (in the next week):

_____

I am looking forward to (in the next six months):

_____

QUICK TIP FOR SALES PROFESSIONALS

After you reach your goal...

What have you given yourself to look forward to? What *will* you give yourself to look forward to?

_____

_____

_____

Stick With It

KEEP SWINGING
Keep swinging your bat

21

"My motto was always to keep swinging. Whether I was in a slump or feeling badly or having trouble off the field, the only thing to do was keep swinging."

Hank Aaron

At the end of the day

At the end of the day, we simply need to keep going.

> "I'd rather be a failure at something I enjoy than be a success at something I hate."
>
> George Burns, actor and comedian

Most goals will yield to persistent effort. Thomas Edison observed, "Genius is 99% perspiration and 1% inspiration."

Three pictures of persistence

As we persist, here are three ways to view our continued efforts.

1. Hold onto the tow rope

Persistence is like holding onto the tow rope in water skiing.

Getting up on skis looks entirely different from *behind* the boat. When watching someone learn to ski from the *inside*, it doesn't look like a big deal. But when we are the one being whipped along from behind, it's a completely different experience. After mustering the nerve to yell, "Hit it!" and having the engine throttled, we get slammed with a wall of water and experience a nasal cleansing for which we were ill-prepared.

Each second is so intense that most people let go of the tow rope after three or four seconds. Many people don't get up because they let go of the rope just one or two seconds too soon.

> *"We want to perfect ourselves so that we can win with less struggle and increasing ease, but the strange thing is that it's not the easy wins we ostensibly seek, but rather the difficult struggles to which we really look forward."*
> Vince Lombardi

When behind the boat, getting up on skis *feels like forever.* In fact, it only takes about *five seconds.*

Regarding your goals, hold onto the rope. Your are likely much closer to reaching your goals than you realize.

2. Stay in the arena

Persistence is like staying in the arena. We're here to live, not to avoid failure. George Burns aptly said, "I'd rather be a failure at something I enjoy than be a success at something I hate."

Theodore Roosevelt was a man who lived passionately "in the arena." His words have inspired thousands to do the same:

"It is not the critic who counts, not the man who points out how the strong man stumbles or where the doer of deeds could have done better. The credit belongs to the man who is actually in the arena, whose face is marred by dust and sweat and blood, who strives valiantly, who errs and comes up short again and again because there is no effort without error and shortcomings, who knows the great devotion, who spends himself in a worthy cause, who at best knows in the end the high achievement of triumph and who, at worst, if he fails while daring greatly, knows his place shall never be with those timid and cold souls who knew neither victory nor defeat."

> *"Obstacles cannot crush me. Every obstacle yields to stern resolve. He who is fixed to a star does not change his mind."*
> Leonardo da Vinci

It is much better to throw ourselves wholly into the adventure of our goals than to timidly hold back in fear of making mistakes. Persisting with our goals is living in the arena.

3. Keep swinging your bat

Even baseball legend Babe Ruth experienced batting slumps. Grantland Rice asked him, "Babe, what do you do when you get in a batting slump?" Ruth replied, "I just keep goin' up there and keep swingin' at 'em. I know the old law of averages will hold good for me the same as it does for anybody else, if I keep havin' my healthy swings. If I strike out two or three times in a game, or fail to get a hit for a week, why should I worry? Let' the pitchers worry; they're the guys who're gonna suffer later on."[1]

For decades he held the record for home runs. He also struck out more times than any other player in history: 1,330 times.

Many years later, Babe Ruth's record was eclipsed by Hank Aaron. Over a 23-year career with the Braves and Brewers, Hammerin' Hank pounded out 755 round-trippers.

He also surpassed Ruth in another important way. He struck out more often. Hank Aaron struck out 53 more times—for a total of 1,383 strikeouts over his career. Aaron's words are reminiscent of Ruth's: "My motto was always to keep swinging. Whether I was in a slump or feeling badly or having trouble off the field, the only thing to do was keep swinging."

Now about your goal. Keep swinging the bat. Keep doing the things you know will get you there.

When you strike out, step back into the batter's box. Swing your bat again.

And again.

And again.

Keep stepping into the batter's box and swinging your bat. The only thing to do is keep swinging.

> *"Few things are impossible to diligence and skill; great works are performed not by strength, but by perseverance."*
> Samuel Johnson

QUICK TIP FOR SALES PROFESSIONALS

Increase your number of "at bats."

What can you do right now to increase your number of "at bats" with prospects?

_____

_____

_____

APPLY: Swing your bat today

Step into the batter's box today. Swing your bat.

What action will you take *today* to keep moving toward your goal?

> What swing will I take today to keep me moving forward?
>
> _____
>
> _____

Thank you

Former British Prime Minister Margaret Thatcher said, "You may have to fight a battle more than once to win it." You and I know this is *certainly* true.

Longfellow wrote, "Those heights by great men, won and kept, were not achieved by sudden flight. But they, while their companions slept, were toiling upward in the night."

I commend you for your hard work and diligence. Like seed planted in the ground, your study and application will reap a harvest in your life.

Thank you for the opportunity to partner together as you pursue your best life!

> *"It's never too late to be what we might have been."*
> George Elliot

Stick With It

REFERENCE NOTES

1 Long-Term

1. *The Magic Lamp*: Keith Ellis (New York: Three Rivers Press, 1996), p. xvii.
2. *Goals!*: Brian Tracy (San Francisco: Berrett-Koehler Publishers, 2003), p. 12.
3. *Lead The Field*: Earl Nightingale (Chicago: Nightingale-Conant Corp., 1986), lecture 11.
4. *Create Your Own Future*: Brian Tracy (Hoboken, NJ: Wiley, 2002), p. 248.

2 Focus

1. *Execution*: Larry Bossidy and Ram Charan (New York: Crown Business, 2002). This insight is shared in several places and ways throughout the book.
2. *Winning:* Jack Welch with Suzy Welch (New York: HarperCollins, 2005), pp. 14-17.

3 Say No

1. *Good To Great*: Jim Collins (New York: HarperCollins, 2001), p. 134.
2. *Today Matters*: John Maxwell (New York: Time Warner Book Group, 2004), p. 286.
3. *Good To Great:* Jim Collins, pp. 128, 136.

4 Act

1. *Create Your Own Future:* Brian Tracy, p. 236.
2. *The Rainmaker:* Jeffrey J. Fox (New York: Hyperion, 2000), p. 111.

5 Now

1. *Organized For Success:* Stephanie Winston (New York: Crown Business, 2004), p. 135.
2. *The Penses:* Blaise Pascal, #47.
3. *How Full Is Your Bucket:* Tom Rath and Donald Clifton (New York: Gallup Press, 2004), p. 53.

6 Self-compete

1. *Wooden:* John Wooden and Steve Jamison (Chicago: Contemporary Books, 1997), p. x.
2. *Wooden:* John Wooden and Steve Jamison, p. vii.
3. *Goal Setting 101:* Gary Ryan Blair (Syracuse, NY: GoalsGuy Learning Systems), p. 11.
4. *Wooden:* John Wooden and Steve Jamison, p. 11.

7 Environment

1. *The Tipping Point:* Malcolm Gladwell (New York: Little, Brown and Company, 2000), p. 165.
2. *Goal Setting 101:* Gary Ryan Blair, p. 28.
3. *Organized For Success:* Stephanie Winston, p. 159.
4. An interesting source of material on this topic can be found in *How to Connect in Business in 90 Seconds or Less:* Nicholas Boothman (New York: Workman Publishing, 2002).
5. *How Full Is Your Bucket:* Tom Rath and Donald Clifton, p. 46.

8 Purpose

1. *Good To Great:* Jim Collins, p 160.
2. *"America's Best Leaders," U.S. News Special Report:* William Meyers, October 31, 2005, p. 50.
3. *Fierce Conversations:* Susan Scott (New York: Viking, 2002).
4. *The Essential Drucker:* Peter Drucker (New York: HarperCollins, 2001), P. 207.

9 Fire

1. Charles Platkin gave this angle on Kennedy's presentation of the space program vision in *Breaking the Pattern* (New York: Red Mill Press, 2002).
2. *The Magic Lamp*: Keith Ellis, p. 4.
3. *A Bias For Action*: Heike Bruch and Sumantra Ghoshal (Boston: Harvard Business School Press, 2004), p. 34.
4. *The Power of Full Engagement*: Jim Lohr and Tony Schwartz (New York: The Free Press, 2003), pp. 174-175.
5. Private conversation with Seth Godin.

11 Small Improvements

1. I have found this story from several sources. The most detailed account is included in Earl Nightingale's *Lead The Field* program.
2. *"The Constant Customer," The Gallup Management online newsletter*: Alec Applebaum, June 17, 2001, http://gmj.gallup.com/content/Default.asp?ci=745&pg=1).
3. *Ideas Are Free*: Alan Robinson and Dean Schroeder (San Francisco: Berrett-Koehler Publishers, 2004), p. 53.
4. Private conversation with Charles Platkin.

12 Momentum

1. *Confidence*: Rosabeth Moss Kanter (New York: Crown Business, 2004), p. 6.
2. *Create Your Own Future*: Brian Tracy, p. 197.
3. *The Magic Lamp*: Keith Ellis, p. 160.
4. *Confidence*: Rosabeth Moss Kanter, p. 45.

13 Habits

1. While this is anonymous, the only place I have found this is in *The Power of Positive Habits*: Dan Robey (Miami: Abritt Publishing Group, p. 2003), p. 35.
2. *The Best Year of Your Life*: Debbie Ford (San Francisco: HarperSanFrancisco, 2005), p. 117.
3. *Breaking the Pattern*: Charles Platkin, p. xiii.
4. *The Power of Full Engagement*: Jim Lohr and Tony Schwartz, p. 167.
5. Private conversation with Tony Schwartz.

14 Big Change

1. *Good To Great*: Jim Collins, p 171.
2. *Notes From A Friend*: Anthony Robbins (New York: Fireside, 1991), p. 31.

Part 3 Overcoming Discouragement

1. *The Best Year of Your Life*: Debbie Ford.

15 Moods

1. *Confidence*: Rosabeth Moss Kanter, p. 40.
2. *Wooden*: John Wooden and Steve Jamison, p. xiii.
3. *Wooden*: John Wooden and Steve Jamison, p. 183.
4. *Wooden*: John Wooden and Steve Jamison, p. 80.

16 Expect

1. *"The Magic Continues," Fortune Magazine*: Brent Schlender, February 3, 2003, p. 123.
2. *"America's Best Leaders," U.S. News Special Report*: Jamie Shreeve, October 31, 2005, p. 70.

3. *"Young carries Texas to the top,"* *USA Today:* Jack Carey, January 5, 2006, p. C1.

17 Be Realistic
1. *Emotional Intelligence:* Daniel Goleman (New York: Bantam Books, 1995), pp. 91-92.
2. *The Art of the Start:* Guy Kawasaki (New York: Portfolio, 2004), p. xi.
3. *The Magic Lamp:* Keith Ellis, p. 201.
4. Private conversation with Jerry Baker.

18 Use Failure
1. *Jack—Straight From The Gut:* Jack Welch and John Byrne (New York: Warner Business Books, 2001), pp. 31-33.

19 Self-Talk
1. *The Scientific American,* September 2003.
2. *Success:* Jena Pinchott (New York: Random House, 2005), p. 209.

20 Energy
1. *The Power of Full Engagement:* Jim Lohr and Tony Schwartz, p. 3.
2. *The Biology of Success:* Robert Arnot (New York: Little, Brown and Company, 2000), pp. 139-140.
3. *Improvise This!:* Mark Bergen, Molly Cox, and Jim Detmar (New York: Hyperion, 2002), p. 116.
4. *The Power of Full Engagement:* Jim Lohr and Tony Schwartz, p. 37.
5. *History of the United States lecture series:* Patrick Allitt, Gary Gallagher, and Allen Guezlo (Chantilly, VA: The Teaching Company, 2nd Edition), lecture on transcontinental railroads.
6. *What They Still Don't Teach You at Harvard Business School:* Mark McCormack (New York: Bantam Books, 1989).

21 Keep Swinging
1. *How I Raised Myself From Success to Failure in Selling:* Frank Bettger (New York: Prentice Hall Press, 1947), p. 181.

THIS PURCHASE HELPS CHARITABLE CAUSES

A portion of the profits from *Stick With It* are being donated to charitable causes. Thank you for making a difference through your purchase of this book.

ACKNOWLEDGEMENTS

First, I want to thank a variety of friends, colleagues, collaborators, customers, and mentors. All of these individuals have played an important role for me in the *Sticking With It* project or content: Steve & Haley Brown, Rob Sample, Doug Heisel, Caleb Couch, Dwayne French, Seth Godin, Tony Schwartz, Charles and Shannon Platkin, Barbara and Elizabeth Pagano, Gary Smith, Lisa Stark, Jerry Baker, Curt & Laurie Altig, John Badostain, Bill Kaplan, John Evans, Gerhard Gschwandtner, Michael & Jennifer Allison, Jason Baker, Caleb Couch, Philip & Julia Carmichael, Craig Hanney, Brian Freese, Rick and Jennifer Kraker, Jude Fouquier, Don Ostrom, and Pastors Wendell and Gini Smith.

I also want to thank Dan Johnson for making the content more impactful through refinement and the adding of ideas where appropriate. Also, thank you to Rosemarie Kowalski, Son Duong, and Roberta Great for your important contributions to text, cover design, and typesetting.

My wife and I greatly appreciate our partners, Ralph and Patty Devin, who have embodied the principle of persistence. They persisted in their support of our vision for our enterprise when it was most needed.

I want to thank my parents, Bill and Kene Wingard, and my wife's parents, Lina and Rick Collins and Rick and Katy Moore. You have instilled these principles in us and you model them to our children.

Most importantly, I am completely indebted to our Executive Producer, Stacy Wingard. You have invested countless hours overseeing every aspect of this project. Your ideas and direction have enabled each project participant to shine, and you have brought all the pieces together in a way that makes the whole greater than the sum of the parts. Without your expertise, skill, and persistence, the dream would not have become a reality.

NOTES
1

NOTES
2

NOTES
3

HELP OTHERS STICK WITH IT!

Get more copies of *Stick With It* for:

- Your sales team
- Your management team
- Your entire organization
- Your group
- Your friends and family members

Order more today by sending in the order form on the next page and mailing it to:

Simple Team Solutions
PMB 438 / 16625 Redmond Way / Suite M
Redmond, WA 98052

Bulk prices here are identical to our online prices (www.stickingwithit.com):

Number	Price
5-19	$13.00/copy
20-99	$12.50/copy
100-499	$11.50/copy
500-999	$11.00/copy
1000-2499	$9.50/copy
2500-4999	$8.50/copy
5000-more	$7.50/copy

Please add 9% for shipping/handling.

Ship to Name (please print)

Ship to Address

Ship to City   State   Zip

email:

Daytime phone:

No. of copies:

Method of payment:
- [ ] Check, Money Order (enclosed)
- [ ] Credit Card

Card Number:

Expiration Date:

Name as it appears on card: (please print)

Signature

Please allow two weeks for delivery.
To contact our office, call 1.877.883.0006.

Thank you for your order!

MORE TOOLS TO HELP YOU STICK WITH IT

1. The audio book, with additional insights and stories by the author

If you like the book, you will *love* the audio book! The author is a highly engaging and motivating communicator. With the audio book you can turn your commute time into growth time and listen to the most impactful chapters over and over again.
Order yours today at www.stickingwithit.com.

2. The free Sticking With It multi-media blog

Following through is a continual journey. Come to www.stickingwithit.com and sign up for Greg's free multi-media blog. On a regular basis he will share his latest findings in video, audio, and print formats.

3. Bring Greg Wingard into your organization

If you want to help your people follow through and go to the next level, bring Greg into your organization as a keynoter.

Greg's unusual ability to connect with people and customize his message makes his presentations remarkably impactful. He keynotes and trains for leading companies as diverse as Microsoft, Disney, and Aflac. Find out Greg's availability by calling the Simple Team Solutions' office at (877) 883-0006.